"We're dealing with a new generation— v
other we've ever seen. We need to h
and get into the battle. Ron has so r
teenagers. May this book ignite the
the fight . . . before it's too late."

Josh
Josh McDowell Ministry

"We can worry and complain about America's young people, or we
can build a bridge into their lives to bring them to Jesus Christ. Ron
is among the best at presenting the gospel to teenagers. We all can
benefit from his experience."

Louis Palau
International Evangelist

"No one speaks more powerfully and more practically on the subject
of reaching youth today than Ron. This book not only outlines the
battle, but also gives a practical strategy you can use to help win the
battle."

Larry Buckland
Billy Graham Evangelistic Association

"Few people have the passion and vision that Ron has for youth. He
is the perfect general with a workable plan to win this battle for a
generation."

Ken Davis
Dynamic Communications

"Everything I see convinces me that a wide-scale revival is coming to
the church and that the youth will be at the forefront. There could be
no more strategic moment for effective youth ministry, and there
surely is no more helpful manual than this book. Don't delay! Let
Ron equip you for the battle . . . and for the victory."

David Bryant
Concerts of Prayer International

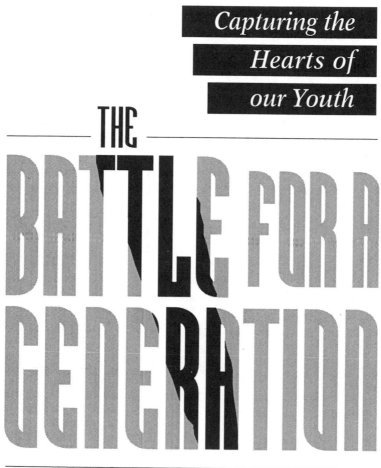

Capturing the
Hearts of
our Youth

THE
BATTLE FOR A
GENERATION

RON HUTCHCRAFT
with Lisa Hutchcraft Whitmer

MOODY PRESS
CHICAGO

All Scripture quotations, unless indicated, are taken from the *Holy Bible: New International Version*. NIV. Copyright © 1973, 1978, 1984 International Bible Society. Used by permission of Zondervan Publishing House. All rights reserved.

Scripture quotations marked NKJV are taken from the *New King James Version*. Copyright © 1979, 1980, 1982, Thomas Nelson, Inc., Publishers. All rights reserved.

ISBN: 0–8024–7131–5

3 5 7 9 10 8 6 4 2

Printed in the United States of America

To

*Those heroic young people who know Jesus Christ, and
who live for Him, no matter what the pressure or the price.*

*". . . Set an example for the believers in speech,
in life, in love, in faith and in purity."*
1 Timothy 4:12

*Those young people who are still unknowingly seeking
a Savior, and whom we pray these pages will help reach.*

*Those concerned, caring adults who have a burden
to be used of God to reach lost and dying young people.*

*"Rescue those being led away to death;
hold back those staggering toward slaughter."*
Proverbs 24:11

CONTENTS

1

THE BATTLE FOR A GENERATION

I t was a thirty-minute stop at a tourist attraction, but what I saw there has pursued me ever since.

Our family was spending a week in an area known to mariners as "The Graveyard of the Atlantic." That name can make you feel a little creepy—it sure wasn't mentioned in the brochures. But not being a seafaring family, the moniker didn't bother us a bit. We loved the wild beauty of that stretch of the Atlantic coast.

The scene is the Outer Banks, a narrow stretch of land off the coast of North Carolina. Because of violent storms, shifting sands, and heavy shipping, the Outer Banks have witnessed hundreds of shipwrecks over the last three centuries. That is why the United States Life Saving Service was so important there in the days before the Coast Guard was born.

The Life Saving Service was, in fact, a spawning ground for heroes. It established its life-saving stations every seven miles along the coast—big white frame buildings, built far enough back from the ocean to be protected from the storms' fury. A few are maintained for tourists today—including the one our family stopped to see in Chicamacomico. (Fortunately, you can go to Chicamacomico without being able to say it.)

During a Park Service demonstration, the period-dressed guides showed us how the station's eight-man crew had carried out rescues. Later I bought a book that described some of those rescues in detail—like the one in which a brutal storm had left four men stranded on a sinking vessel with only the mast above the water. The Life Saving crew members stood on the beach, contemplating the limited chances of their own little boat surviving the three-mile trip to the site of the sinking ship. The chances were good that they themselves might be swept out to sea. But they went anyway—after each one left a verbal will with the one man who stayed behind to man the station.

They went for twenty-two hours without food or sleep, they worked for eight battered hours against the storm . . . and they brought back all four men alive! In another storm—called the worst of the nineteenth century—a single Life Saving crewman plunged right into the violent surf to help people going down on a sinking ship offshore. He battled his way through the surf and the storm to bring back one survivor alive, then another, and another. By the time he collapsed in exhaustion on the beach, he had single-handedly rescued all ten people aboard. Exploits like these put flesh on the courageous motto of the Life Saving Service—"You have to go out. You don't have to come back."

I was deeply affected by what I had seen and heard at the Life Saving Station. Not just because of a glimpse into brave maritime history. But because I knew, as I stood alone on the porch of that old rescue station, that I had seen something much more personal. I had seen a vivid picture of what it means to rescue lost young people today from the storm and surf that are destroying so many.

The rescue effort begins when we *hear the cries of dying people*. The heroes of the Life Saving Service knew their efforts were life-or-death. They plunged into the storm and the surf because they knew the people out there were dying. It is that sense of urgency that will ultimately compel an individual or a church to *do* something about the lost young people around them.

Even secular researchers realize the critical situation our kids are in. Several years ago, some major research was done on American teenagers. The researchers were so alarmed by their findings that they entitled their report "Code Blue." When my wife was in the hospital for surgery recently, the button next to her bed had those two words over it. In a medical environment, a "Code Blue" is a summons to all personnel that this is a life-or-death emergency—one for which everyone drops what he or she is doing to respond. That is how the researchers described the desperation of American teenagers. Drop everything . . . respond quickly . . . this is life-or-death.

Does that describe the attitude of your church or your organization to the needs of young people? Are you in a "Code Blue" mode, marshaling an urgent, aggressive response to teenage lostness? Even people without an understanding of spiritual lostness can see the danger our kids are in. Surely God's people must be mobilized for the emergency.

A DROWNING GENERATION

The numbers are staggering: Suicide among children ages ten to fourteen has increased 120 percent in twelve years[1] . . . one out of three American teenagers has considered suicide and one out of seven has attempted it[2] . . . the homicide rate among fourteen to seventeen year olds has increased 165 percent in ten years[3] . . . marijuana use has almost doubled in two years . . . and alcohol use among minors has been described by a former surgeon general as "out of control."[4] The statistics documenting the crisis are virtually endless. Each one has a name, someone's son or daughter, a priceless creation of God. Thousands of young people are drowning in the storm. Someone has to care enough to hear their cries.

If I were to summarize the lostness of today's kids in a few words, I would describe them as:

Tormented by Loneliness

In my thirty-three years of working with young people, I have never known so many to feel so alone—so willing to do anything to keep from feeling alone for a little while.

Controlled by Sex

No generation has ever grown up amid the sex-saturated bombardment these kids have faced from early ages. It seems almost impossible for many of them to go even a few minutes without sexual thoughts.

Fascinated with Satan

Satanic themes, symbols, and darkness run all through much of their music and many of their videos. One young man summed it up to me—"Kids in our school think Satan is a lot more interesting than God."

Used to Suicide

They are the first generation to grow up with the words "teenage" and "suicide" linked as if they go together. Most young people know that the suicide door is open if things get painful enough.

As I stood on that Life Saving Station porch, I could almost picture a storm-driven sea out there and the desperate cries of dying people. The cries need to be heard by a new breed of rescuers. The cries come from kids who are trying to face the storm without Jesus. The rescuers are adults who know Jesus.

THE RESCUE PLAN

The Life Saving visit also reminded me of a basic rescue principle: Dying people will not come to the Life Saving Station to be rescued. The rescuers have to leave the comfort of the station and go where the dying people are. Never in the history of the Life Saving Service did a drowning person come to the door of the station asking, "Would you please rescue me?" In every case, someone had to leave the safety of the station to save lives.

Today, our life-saving station probably has a steeple with a cross on top. The title of the life-saving talk is on a sign out front, along with the name of the Head Rescuer. Inside, people are singing life-saving songs and having life-saving committee meetings. The station is a great place for the rescuers to have their needs met, their strength built. And it is the best place to bring people after they are saved. But it is *not* the best place to rescue people. In fact, when it comes to lost teenagers, most will probably not come to our life-saving station. If we wait until they do, most of them will die.

Youth ministry, Jesus-style, requires the courage to leave our comfort zone and plunge into the surf and the storm—as He did. Our rescue efforts will take us into places that are not comfortable, into methods that may not be understood, into a youth culture that is out of control.

But that is where the kids are who are dying emotionally and spiritually.

In a sense, our work is not even youth ministry. It is *war.* A battle rages for a generation of young people—and the winner owns the future.

I am convinced that the forces of darkness are trying to spiritually neutralize one generation of teenagers so that generation belongs to them. If they can capture one generation, they can have all the others that come from it. That generation may well be in our schools right now.

A generation is spiritually neutralized when . . .

The lost kids know almost nothing about Jesus.

The "found" kids are not living for Jesus.

Certainly we are facing a majority of teenagers today who are almost spiritually illiterate, with little or no knowledge of the Bible or morality. And it is difficult to find Christian young people who are living at school on Monday what they claimed to believe on Sunday. The devil's goal seems to be within his reach—a generation he effectively controls.

But the forces of darkness are no match for the force of Jesus Christ: "You . . . have overcome them, because the one who is in you is greater than the one who is in the world" (1 John 4:4).

Then how come the darkness seems to be winning our young people? *The forces of Christ have not shown up for the battle.* This is a time for the full mobilization of God's people to rescue dying young people. A battle rages for a generation, and if we do not join the battle, we forfeit a generation. Our call to arms is the cries of lost kids. Calling us to take the risks to rescue them. Calling us to war.

Anyone who touches the life of a teenager will be involved in this war. Every one of us ought to pick up a gun and join this battle, whether we have children of our own, lead a youth ministry, or know any teenagers in our towns. Warfare strategies are not theoretical; it's time to practice active warfare.

It is vital that the church be mobilized for this battle. I know of no cause that will unite and ignite a local congregation faster than saying, "We are going to fight for the kids in this town." It's the one cause the church as a whole can all agree on, because today's kids are front-page news. Those kids who are drowning in the surf have no advocate back at the life-saving station. Maybe you will become their advocate and say, "We cannot leave them lost." The devil is throwing everything he's got—billions of dollars, the best talent he can find, and the most attractive packages he can create—to win this generation. If this generation is lost, it won't be because he's more powerful than we are or has something better to offer. It will be because we didn't show up. We won't lose by fighting. We will lose by forfeit.

The war for young people begins with an understanding of teenage lostness. The kids of today are a product of a process that has been eroding their souls since "teenagers" began.

FOUR DEADLY DECADES

I have a dictionary from 1943. In that dictionary the word *teenager* does not appear. If you were between twelve and twenty years old, you were simply an older child or young adult.

There were two great explosions at the end of the Second World War. One was the atomic bomb, and the other was the *birth of the youth culture*. Both had a huge impact on our world. All of a sudden, our country and world were faced with a culture within a culture. Every parent knew there was something different—different values, different heroes, different music, different vocabulary. Overnight, parents were thinking, "I don't understand this person who is my child."

Suddenly, the church of Jesus Christ was faced with an awesome challenge, because we had a separate youth culture within our culture, and we had to figure out a way to cross cultures to reach them. For more than thirty years of youth ministry, I have been a cross-cultural missionary without leaving my country. Youth culture is not an extension of the adult culture. It is *another* culture.

There have always been young people, but there have been four decisive decades of the youth *culture*—the fifties, sixties, seventies, and eighties. The young people of the nineties are the product of those turbulent decades. I believe there has been an unfolding of a satanic strategy for capturing a generation, because in each of those decades, kids were stripped of something essential to growing up whole.

Loss of Innocence

In the 1950s, kids lost their *innocence*. This loss of innocence has continued ever since. Back in the fifties when I was a teenager, there was a Judeo-Christian consensus in America on what was right and wrong. Did people ever do the wrong thing? Yes. Did they feel like they had? Yes. There was a sense of people all agreeing that something was right, and something was wrong, even if they didn't all live what was right. There was also a general awareness in our culture of Christian teachings, Bible stories, and Bible characters.

That Judeo-Christian consensus started to waver in the 1950s. One of the greatest things that contributed to the loss of innocence was the birth of television. I remember the day my dad brought home this little box with a seven-inch black-and-white screen. My mom and I were glued to it. Imagine watching "I Love Lucy" *before* it was a rerun. TV was a revolutionary development and people couldn't turn it off. They still can't.

Television brought about a revolution that is described in Neil Postman's book *The Disappearance of Childhood*. Postman points out that before the emergence of television, children had to learn to read before they discovered "the secrets of adulthood."[5] Until you could read about something or were told about it, you didn't know about it. TV changed all that. Instantly.

A five year old's innocence is assaulted every day through TV, either during a show or in the ads for the next show. Parents find themselves trying to answer a young child asking questions such as, "Mommy, what's rape? Daddy, what's a prostitute?" Innocence cannot last long when a child only has to push a button to be deluged with darkness.

The music of these four decades is a thermometer of the growing loss of innocence in the youth culture. As early as the 1950s, a song like the Everly Brothers' "Wake Up, Little Susie" was suggesting that a couple had spent most of the night together. But this was only the beginning of seeing the music pollution of young people. Today—reinforced by the driving visual images of music videos—popular songs freely portray promiscuous sex, satanic darkness, violent anger, and open blasphemy. The erosion of innocence began when the youth culture was born in the 1950s. Today, innocence is only a memory.

Loss of Authority

In the 1960s, kids lost their *authority*. The 1960s brought a turbulent time when every authority was challenged, whether it was the teacher in the classroom, the parent in the home, the president in the White House, or God in heaven. Rooted in the rebellion of the sixties is the prevailing attitude that "Nobody can tell me what's right or wrong." Under an abused concept of "tolerance," the words *right* and *wrong* have been banished from the classroom for decades. Talk shows wallow daily in the swamp of lifestyles spawned by "no authority but me."

Consequently, there is now a generation of people who not only don't know what right and wrong are, but don't even know there *is* such a thing as right or wrong. Today's young people are playing on a field with no boundaries. If you tried that in soccer or football, you would have *chaos*—not to mention demoralized officials. You can't have a game without boundaries—and you certainly can't have a life without them. But today's young people are trying to. And they are out of control.

Because so many young people believe in *nothing*, they can be made to believe in *anything*—whether it's a cult, New Age mysticism, or satanic darkness. They have nothing by which to measure truth. They have lost their authority.

Loss of Lovedness

Another deadly blow to growing up whole came as the next decade unfolded. In the 1970s, kids lost their *lovedness*, that sense of feeling loved, of feeling valuable. With Mom and Dad either trying to keep their marriage together or take it apart, there wasn't much left for their children. The divorce statistics continued to spiral upward in the seventies. Even in many undivided families, both parents went to work to keep up with burgeoning expenses and, in some cases, to try to find identity in a career. Consequently, in the 1970s we began to hear about "latch-key children," and since then there have been more and more kids coming home to an empty house—to be raised by video games, talk show hosts, and MTV. And "home alone," they were not getting much affirmation, communication, or affection. This left many kids feeling unloved, unnoticed, uncared for, and neglected.

At the same time in the 1970s, there was a tremendous growth in the amount of sexual activity among young people. It had as much to do with a desire for intimacy as it did biology. For many kids, twenty minutes of sex was the closest thing to feeling loved they ever felt. Tragically, they did not realize the emotional, relational, and physical price tag. All they knew was that it seemed like a few minutes of love. Loneliness has made many young people dangerously vulnerable to sexual mistakes and peer pressure— "anything for love."

Loss of Hope

With innocence, authority, and "lovedness" lost, there was only one treasure left to lose. In the 1980s, young people lost their *hope*. As we watched the suicide statistics grow, we found kids saying, "Why should I stick around? It's not going to get any better." There is only one age group in America where the death rate is rising, and that is among teenagers. Seventy-eight percent of the kids who die in this country die a violent death, whether from homicide, suicide, or a traffic accident. These deaths are often caused by drinking or drugs.

In the past twenty years, hope has disappeared, while suicide has doubled among fifteen to nineteen year olds. Suicide has also tripled among ten to fourteen year olds. At the same time, homicide has doubled among ten to fourteen year olds.

Often, in the suburbs the issue is suicide and in the city the issue is homicide. In the suburbs where kids have a lot, they grow up on top of the mountain everybody else is trying to climb. Those trying to climb "Mt. Prosperity" say, "If we can get to the top of the mountain, we'll be happy." Kids who grew up on the top of the mountain say, "There's nothing here"—and they jump off. In the city where kids aren't rich, they're killing each other in an effort to reach the top. But both violent choices are saying, "What's the use—there's no hope."

USA Today once reported that one in seven American teenagers has attempted suicide. Sadly, that survey was taken among eighth and tenth graders . . . younger teenagers. One-third of the kids interviewed said they had seriously considered suicide.[6] So many young people—more than we know—are thinking about dying.

Four deadly decades—since there have been "teenagers," they have been losing what they cannot live without. Those four decades have created the young people of the nineties, who are "loster" than kids have ever been. One newspaper summed it up in a front-page article that says:

> Adolescence in America has become a deadly mine field. And increasing numbers of young people are not making it through. Some perish along the way, killing themselves, murdering one another or dying in accidents. Others emerge wounded, bearing physical or emotional scars that they will carry for the rest of their lives.
>
> Doctors now refer to the "new morbidity" of adolescence, recognizing that risk-taking behavior presents extremely grave threats to teenagers. And there are those who, while they are still children, default on their futures, squander educational opportunities because of drug use, who contract sexually-transmitted diseases, who break the law and end up with police or prison records, who become pregnant or are forced into premature parenthood.
>
> Figures from the National Center for Health Statistics give a grim picture of the growing risks of adolescence.
>
> • Every 78 seconds, an adolescent in this country attempts suicide. Every 90 minutes one succeeds.
>
> • Every 20 minutes an adolescent is killed in an accident. Every 80 minutes one is murdered.

• Every 31 seconds an adolescent becomes pregnant.

• Nearly half of all high school seniors have used an illegal drug at least once and almost 90% have used alcohol, some on a daily basis.[7]

Even unbelievers in our society are alarmed. This is Code Blue. Has the world seen the lostness of kids before the church has? It is time for us to wake up. We have the answer. All the world can do is document the problem and cite the statistics. We who have the answer need to hear the wake-up call. Reaching young people is a life-or-death issue.

But there is also some hope-filled *good* news about young people, too. They are more *ready for Jesus* than they have ever been. They don't know they're ready for Jesus; they just know they're ready for *something*. If teenagers feel your authentic love and hear you present Jesus properly, they will respond to this Savior who is *everything* their hearts are hungry for. That is the hope.

1. Kim Painter, "Suicide Among Young Teens Increases 120%" *USA Today,* 21 April 1995, 70.
2. Nanci Hellmich, "1 in 7 Teens Say They've Tried Suicide," *USA Today,* September 1988.
3. Robert Davis, "Crime Study Details 'Young and Ruthless,' " *USA Today,* September 1995.
4. John Elson, "Drink Until You Finally Drop," *Time,* 16 December 1991, 64–65.
5. Neil Postman, *The Disappearance of Childhood* (New York: Vintage, 1994).
6. Hellmich, "1 in 7 Teens."
7. Ronald Kotulak, "Today's Adolescents Are Dealing with Different Choices and Greater Risks," *Chicago Tribune,* 7 December 1986. Used by permission.

2

12 Sentences That Define a Generation

Y ou have just walked into your doctor's office. Before you can even tell him why you have come, he says to the nurse, "Penicillin!" Then, much to your dismay, he begins to prepare your injection. He has not listened to your symptoms. He knows nothing about your condition. But he is quick to offer a treatment.

It is obvious that the young people around us are in urgent need of a cure for their desperation, pain, and lostness. But before we begin to treat them, we must understand where they hurt and the underlying causes of their "symptoms." Before we can begin to develop an efficient strategy for changing their lives, it is important that we understand the young people we want to reach.

Businesses do market research before they present their products to find out "Who are we selling to?" A missionary doesn't parachute into Irian Jaya and say, "Hello, natives. Let me speak to you about my Jesus." No, he spends a long time in language study and learning about the culture. He learns about the things he should and should not say. He learns why they do what they do, plus what things are sacred and important to that people group.

UNDERSTANDING THE NATIVES

Since we are missionaries to another culture, we need to begin by understanding the natives we are trying to reach. Their lives and needs can be summed up in twelve sentences that define this generation.

Loneliness Is Their Heart Condition

If there is one word other than lost to describe young people today, it would be the word *lonely*. They are desperately lonely people.

One of the reasons for this deep loneliness is that kids have largely grown up alone. They go home to an empty house, where they are raised by the flickering blue parent called TV. They spend hours and hours alone in the little kingdoms called their bedrooms. More than any other generation, today's young people have had to raise *themselves* without meaningful relationships around them.

Faculty members with University of Chicago Behavioral Science Department did a study on thousands of teenagers a few years ago. They gave each teenager a signaling device. When it signaled them, they were supposed to write down what they were thinking or feeling at that time. The teenagers were "signaled" during the day, during the night, while they were at school, while they were alone. One of the researchers' primary conclusions was that today's teenagers appear to be almost terrified of being alone. For when they are alone, it is almost as if they do not exist.

It's no wonder a teenager has to call someone on the phone as soon as he or she gets home from school. He or she saw that person fifteen minutes ago. What could have possibly happened in those fifteen minutes that would necessitate a phone call? A call expresses this feeling that, "I'm alone. I don't exist. Quick, get me somebody so I exist."

One of the reasons that young people are so lonely is that they have had little relationship practice. Communication is hard for them. The family setting of previous generations didn't have all the distractions of Walkmans™, video games, and TV. Guess what people learned to do then? Talk.

Today's kids are not great conversationalists. Communication comes hard to people who have not had much practice—so their relationships tend to be superficial. They talk about trivial, surface subjects that are pretty meaningless and do not create real closeness.

A parent of a teenager might say, "It seems like they're talking to each other all the time. Look at my phone bill!" Although there is a lot of talk, there isn't much communication. Subjects are usually superficial, such as what was on TV last night, who is going out with whom, sports, "social soap operas" among their peers, schoolwork, etc. When it comes to sustained, substantial discussion of feelings and ideas, today's young people are sadly crippled.

Consequently, since teenagers often do not know how to express what they are feeling, they can be *explosive* people. Just because they do not *express* their feelings doesn't mean they don't *feel* them deeply. When all these explosive feelings build up inside, they can push a young person to violent or self-destructive choices. Feelings build up because kids think there is no one to talk to—and because they do not know how to express feelings. All of this increases and intensifies their loneliness.

When talking with young people, it's clear that it is hard for them to put their feelings into words. They seem scared to do it. When I tape my youth radio broadcast "Alive! with Ron Hutchcraft," I interact with a studio audience of teenagers. Many youth pastors will bring their kids in to participate, and they often say, "I've never heard my kids talk like this." It may be because we have them write down their thoughts first, then they express what they have already written down. They are used to being with themselves—so it feels safer to write it down and *then* possibly to say it. But communication is very, very hard for these lonely people.

Teenagers are vulnerable sexually, because sex offers brief intimacy. For many of them, brief intimacy is more than they have ever had. The problem is that then they have given away what they can never get back—their virginity. They often come away more disillusioned than ever, feeling more used than loved. While they received a few minutes of feeling physically close to someone, they found out it did not give them love—so another hope has let them down. They become disappointed in their relationships and starved for a loving feeling.

Although this loneliness is an open door through which counterfeit love can come, it is also a door through which *Christ's* love can enter. The adult who wants to attract and affect young people must first provide *an atmosphere in which they feel loved*. If you love them, they almost don't care what you believe.

One time after speaking at a church in New York City, I met a girl who wandered in, who had never attended the church before. She mentioned she was about to join a particular cult. After asking more questions, I learned she had grown up in an evangelical church and knew a lot of biblical truth. When I asked her if she really believed this cult leader's teachings, she said, "Well, to be honest with you, I think about 90 percent of what he teaches is [expletive deleted]."

I said, "And you're about to sign your life on with them? Why?"

She said, "Because for the first time in my life I went to a place where I felt cared for and loved."

Today's teenager is not asking the biblical question, "What must I do to be saved?" He or she is asking, "What must I do to be *loved?*" Teens will go where the love is.

In 1975, the face of a seventeen-year-old redhead suddenly appeared on every front page in America. Her name was Lynette "Squeaky" Fromme. Squeaky was a follower of mass murderer Charles Manson, and she may be in prison the rest of her life because of that allegiance. After the assassination attempt on President Gerald Ford, an interviewer asked Squeaky why she had committed herself to Charles Manson. She answered, "When I was about 14 years old, I realized I was a misfit. I was a misfit at home and at school, so I left home. I ran across the country, ending up sitting on a curb in Whittier, California. A man came up to me, put his hand on my head and said, 'Come with me and I will take care of you.' And I believed him, so I followed him. His name was Charles Manson." She said, "I would still die for him." Verbalizing what most teenagers today feel, she said, "I decided when I was 14 years old that whoever loved me first could have my life."[1]

We drive or walk by thousands of Squeakys in our lifetimes. They are all around our churches, our towns. *Whoever loves them first will have them!*

Relationships Matter Most to Them

The number-one priority for modern young people is relationships. They will do almost anything to get one—and then to keep it. When a young person gets something that looks like it might be a decent relationship, he or she will pay almost any price for it.

Relationships have become number one because *deprivation creates value.* Whatever you are deprived of is what you tend to value. For example, the depression generation in this country values what they didn't have—houses, cars, jobs, money. They made sure their kids would have all of that, but the generations that have followed value something different that *they* haven't had.

In order for Mom and Dad to get the cars, house, money, and clothes, they had to leave the kids. Consequently, the kids of recent generations have been deprived of a *relationship.* They have been deprived of closeness and love, belonging and relationships, so they'll do anything for closeness.

When I speak at Christian colleges, I try to talk to the administrators and deans of the campus and learn from them. On every campus I have visited, I've asked, "What has changed in the last ten years among the students here?"

I have heard different answers, but one almost always comes up: "Dysfunction." Christian college leaders have said, "We have never before seen this much dysfunction. These are children of dysfunction. Abused, hurt, children of divorce, children of alcoholics, children of all kinds of dysfunctional problems." The Christian college scene is evidence of what's going on in the youth culture and what's going on in the church. Once again, relationships have been unsatisfying, so they're looking for a close relationship.

Another change in the young relationship scene is that they used to like having a "crowd"—a large circle of friends. But now kids tend to only have two or three close people with whom they do everything. Young people would like to have a lot of friends, but they put about 80 percent of their social eggs in a basket of two or three kids. So it is easy to get hurt.

My wife and I used to answer questions for a teen column in a magazine, and we always had a large number of questions asking, "What do I do if my best friend is drifting away from me?" The desperation hits because they have counted so heavily on one or two friends. They have few close friends, and those few relationships matter tremendously.

An adult who is willing to be a trusted friend can profoundly influence a teenager's life—especially if that adult can point a teenager to the only Relationship that will fill the hole in his heart.

Music Is Their Language

Sometimes on a Saturday night I can pick up an exciting radio program called "¡Chévere!" (that's Spanish for "cool"). It's actually the Spanish version of our ministry's youth broadcast, "Alive!" I hear it on short-wave from Latin America. It has all the ingredients I use in "Alive!"—music, drama, interaction with a live studio audience of teenagers, biblical straight talk. There's just one problem. I can barely understand a word they're saying. But "¡Chévere!" isn't trying to reach Anglos like me. We are talking Missions 101 here—you communicate your message in the language of the people you are trying to reach.

The youth culture today has its own vocabulary, heroes, fashions, lifestyle—a fact every parent of a teenager knows all too well. Any adult who hopes to present Christ in that culture must do what every missionary does—speak the language of the native.

The language of young people today is their *music*. They receive thousands of messages—most of them sub-Christian or anti-Christian—through their music. That music comes in many forms—rock, rap, heavy metal, alternative, and whatever new derivative may develop next week.

When I was a teenager in the "Happy Days" 1950s, Elvis and the Everly Brothers were important to us. But today, music is much more than important to teenagers—it is a major part of their *identity*. They are fiercely opinionated about it—one of the few things they care enough about to have a strong opinion. Some research shows that, given a list of fifty-four "coping options" for problem times, kids rank music number one. One popular rock star said, "When I was in high school, music was my best friend."

It is hard for us as adults to imagine music so totally taking over a young person's thinking and identity. But we adults do not get to vote on this—music *is* the language of the generation we need so desperately to reach.

After listening to some current songs, many adults might ask, "You call that music?" Much of it sounds like screaming. But music expresses what is in our souls. What is in the soul of a younger generation who carry a suitcase full of pain is anger, hurt, and pent-up frustration. That "dysfunctional music" expresses the dysfunction in their soul. That screaming singer is screaming their scream. For contemporary young people, their music and their souls are tightly intertwined.

This understanding is important for a man or woman who wants to affect a teenager's life.

First, we need to know that when we attack a young person's music, we are attacking the young person—at least that's how it feels to the teenager. Many a son or daughter has been painfully alienated by a parental tirade against his or her music. Is music too important to young people? Yes. But while we do not agree with its importance to them, we cannot ignore it in trying to reach them.

In addition, as we try to communicate Christ to a generation whose language is certain styles of music, we are faced with some difficult choices. Shall we eliminate these contemporary styles of music from our youth ministry tool kit because they have been so corrupted by the darkness? Or shall we use the language of the natives to communicate the Light? These are delicate, sometimes divisive issues.

But fundamentally, caring Christian adults must think of music as a missionary would think—and consider the impact of Jesus coming into kids' lives through the language they know best.

I didn't ask Spanish-speaking kids to learn English because I am more comfortable with that language. I knew I had to put God's truth in a language I did not speak so they would hear and understand. Missionaries speak the language of the people they are trying to reach, not vice versa.

Self-Worth Is Their Struggle

Life is busy at the Hutchcraft house, so mealtime sometimes has to be paper plate time. When we've inhaled our hamburgers or pizza, we trash our paper plates. We never wash those plates or save them for another feast. They're only worth a penny or two, so we throw them out. Guilt-free.

Then there's our fine china. Now that's a different story. It's not super-expensive, but it's our "nice stuff." You can usually visit those dishes in their special cabinet in the dining room. We keep china there for special occasions, like Thanksgiving or Christmas. We *do* wash it when we're finished. We *don't* throw it away. Why? Because it's too valuable to throw away.

Tragically, most young people today feel like paper plates, and they are throwing themselves away. People can throw themselves away sexually, chemically, alcoholically, academically. They can throw themselves away by having no goals and by the friends they choose. Much of what we are seeing as "the problems of teenagers today," and even the ultimate discarding of lives with suicide, is ultimately from kids who are saying, "I don't matter. I'm cheap. I'm not worth much. It doesn't matter what I do to myself. If I could just feel better for a little while."

It doesn't matter what you do to a paper plate. So when we tell young people, "Don't do that to yourself" and "You should just say no," they think, "Why? I'm not worth anything. It doesn't matter what I do with something worthless." Often they look at their future and say, "What future? I'm not going to have much of a future anyway."

The Bible contains transforming news about a person's

worth—"We are *God's workmanship*" (Ephesians 2:10, italics added). God didn't make any paper plates. He only made fine china. But until kids believe they're fine china, they'll keep throwing themselves away. Many of the "problems of youth" are actually only *symptoms*. The problem is often *self-worth*, surfacing in throwaway behaviors such as alcohol abuse, sexual involvement, and occult activity.

What has happened to make young people with great God-given worth feel and act so worthless? One contributing factor is *unavailable parents*. The fundamental source for people to get their "I'm valuable" messages is from a mom or dad who is there to frequently affirm them, hug them, listen to them, and tell them they're doing OK.

Second, a young person's worth can be damaged by parents' high-performance expectations. Many mothers and fathers want their kids to be "super kids." So they push their children into cheerleading, activities, sports, clubs—and into a "premature maturity."

Many parents unwittingly attach their ego to their child's performance, "He gets an 'A'; I get an 'A'." "She wins; I win." This helps explain those little league games where parents seem to need a sedative. What's happening? Well, that's *me* playing. He strikes out; I strike out. He gets a hit; I get a hit. He pitches a no-hitter; I pitch a no-hitter. The pressure to perform is intense—and any failure takes a heavy toll on a child or teenager's confidence. Because the parents have attached their ego to kids in this highly competitive, performance-oriented society, kids' shortcomings are often talked about, but seldom their achievements; their weaknesses are addressed, but not their strengths. Most young people aren't sure what's right about them; they only know what they need to work on.

The school scene often leaves a teenager feeling smaller too. At school, it is cool to be cruel. As relationships have deteriorated and communication has diminished, put-downs have become almost an art form among young people. Once a kid hits junior high, school is a social shark tank. If there's anything wrong with him, his peers will find it and attack it. Most kids are either too skinny or too fat, too tall or too short, too smart or too dumb—too something. Hair, teeth, hips, nose—everything is a potential target. This verbal cruelty tears down teenagers' confidence and focuses them on their negative traits. The feelings of "paper plate" worthlessness get almost daily reinforcement.

Media images also erode a teenager's self-image. They are

constantly getting pumped with what they're "supposed to" look like. Teenage girls pick up magazines and they see pictures of beautiful girls. They compare themselves in the mirror with them and say, "Yuck. I don't look like that."

Of course, there is a little secret about that glamorous image. First, magazines get just the right model for the right job. She has dieted to a weight that is probably unhealthy for her and perhaps had plastic surgery as well. The studios take her in and work several hours to do the perfect make-up job, create the perfect hair style, and get the perfect clothes from the wardrobe department. They put her under perfect lighting. They take 150 continuous-frame photos of her. Then they pick the one in which she really looks good. They airbrush that photo and take all the imperfections out of it. Teenage girls look at that and say, "I don't look like that." Well, the *model* doesn't even look like that! This woman doesn't exist. But meanwhile the poor teenage girl says, "Look at me. Ick."

The impact of teenagers' self-image on their behavior cannot be underestimated. A caring Christian adult brings wonderful news for them. In Psalm 139:13–14, David says, "For you created my inmost being; you knit me together in my mother's womb. I praise you because I am fearfully and wonderfully made; your works are wonderful." That prayer is saying, "Lord, You only make master-pieces and You made me. I am a unique, one-of-a-kind, hand-made creation of God." Like the Mona Lisa, every person is a priceless masterpiece, signed by the Artist.

We must begin to build "fine china" kids by showing them that their worth is based not on their appearance, achievement, or acceptance, but on who designed them. There is no one they can be compared with—they are originals.

Teenagers cannot find their incalculable worth until they realize who they were made by and made for (Colossians 1:16), and how much God spent to pay for them. They have been made by God and paid for by God at the cost of His Son. Romans 5:8 says, "But God demonstrates his own love for us in this: While we were still sinners, Christ died for us." At times I have challenged a teenager to go to the Cross and look at the price being paid for him there—and then tell me he is nobody.

Anesthetic Is More Important Than Cure

Kids are often not as interested in a solution to their problem as they are in getting the pain to stop. They have no idea how to deal with the pressure or problem that has come—so they think their only hope is to feel good for awhile. "Give me an anesthetic." "Dull the pain." It does not occur to them that there might be a cure. Cures take a little work and a little time. Pain relievers solve nothing, but they're easy and quick.

What are some of the sedatives young people use? Music sedates them. Drugs can sedate them. A party. Drinking. When kids commit suicide, it is not usually because they want to die; it's because *they want the pain to stop.*

In light of the pain so many young people carry, there is much hope in a Savior who says, "Come to me, all you who are weary and burdened, and I will give you rest" (Matthew 11:28). Christ puts problems into perspective when He says, "In this world you will have trouble. But take heart! I have overcome the world" (John 16:33). He shows us we can win because "in all these things, we are more than conquerors through him who loved us" (Romans 8:37).

For a world of hurting teenagers, we have something far better than a sedative for the pain. We have in Jesus Christ a *cure.* Kids who have been trying to outrun their pain can finally stop running. There is a Burden-Bearer, a Savior to walk with them from pain into hope.

They Know No Boundaries

Because authority was lost back in the sixties, today's young people play on a field without boundaries. Can you imagine a football game on a field with no boundaries? Picture a player carrying the ball who is about to be tackled—so he tries a new game plan. Suddenly the runner leaps over the bench on the sideline, knocks over three cheerleaders, and heads for the stands. He is in the fourteenth row, and he's running for a touchdown. The officials are down on the field asking each other, "What do you think? Think he's out of bounds yet?"

Since there is no sense of right or wrong, they have no sense of sin. If there are no boundaries, how can you be out of bounds? This presents a difficult challenge for presenting the Gospel. How do you show the need for a Savior to someone to whom sin is a non-issue?

How do you present a Savior to a generation that doesn't think sin is a problem? There is an effective way. It involves sharing an unchanged message but with a different starting point. This will be discussed in a later chapter.

But as we work to understand the young people around us,

we need to remember they are products of a culture that knows no boundaries. We cannot assume anything about their understanding of Christian morality.

We have to start out morally basic, even with the church kids who may have heard what we said, but it has never sunk in. It is amazing how much mail our ministry receives from church kids who listen to "Alive! with Ron Hutchcraft" who say they never really understood that sex before marriage was wrong. I know they don't teach anything different in their churches, but somehow it has never registered for many church kids that there is such a thing as a moral line for when you have sex.

We see boundaries when we walk on the playing field; most young people do not. If we are going to have a life-changing impact on them, we will have to first show them there *are* boundaries . . . explain why boundaries are good . . . and then explain where God has drawn the lines.

They Want Authority

Back in the sixties and early seventies, before you could say anything to a group of young people, you had to have a big discussion. It was important to start off saying, "Now how do *you* feel?" There was a desire for a lot of dialogue. Then maybe in the last five minutes you could present biblical truth.

Today teenagers still want to share their feelings, but they're saying, "I want *answers*, not questions. Will somebody tell me what's true, what's right?" They are looking for authority—but it is authority that is earned, not demanded. A position—whether that of pastor, parent, youth leader, teacher—does not automatically give an adult authority in their lives.

In previous generations, if you had the badge, you had the authority. People respected and listened to the sheriff, president, parents, teacher, reverend. Nowadays, titles mean little. For one thing, too many people have devalued the titles with scandal and hypocrisy. No, effective authority in young people's lives is not demanded—it is *earned*. You earn authority by listening to them, loving them, spending time with them. And they are looking for someone who is worthy of trust. They want answers. They also want boundaries, but they haven't found many people they trust to help them find the lines.

Positional authority—authority derived from the position you hold—does not mean much to kids today. But *personal* authority—the kind that comes from the kind of *person* you are—is exactly what their questioning hearts are looking for. They're tired of no boundaries, no answers. They are truly "sheep without a shepherd" (Matthew 9:36).

Their Now Matters More Than Their Future

"The future is too far off—and it may never come"—that's the unspoken feeling behind many young choices. Spiritually, modern kids are not particularly concerned about going to heaven or particularly afraid of going to hell. That's not real—it's out there somewhere.

Sadly, a common thing that you will hear from lost teenagers when you talk about hell is, "Well, my friends are going there." That's the ultimate expression of "I don't care where I am as long as my friends are there. My friends are number one." How tragic—especially in light of Jesus' portrayal of the aloneness of hell (Luke 16:19–31).

Teenagers live in the present, so they're saying, "Hell—that doesn't matter to me. I've got to live with my parents. I've just got to get through this week. I have to handle this pressure. I was so depressed last night . . . maybe that's hell. I don't know." A spiritual case that is focused on the future—gaining heaven, avoiding hell—will not be persuasive for many kids who are mired in their now.

It is often ineffective to say, "The reason you need to do what Jesus says is because five years from now it will make a difference." They think, "So, when is five years from now?" For a teenager, a week seems like an eternity. Their unspoken question is, "What difference will this make *now?*" When trying to present the Gospel to a young person, it is important to answer that question.

Yes, the future implications of their decisions need to be discussed with teenagers—we do not serve them well if we allow them to forget the future. But we must also be sure to address the present, to *begin* with the now they care about, not the future they don't care about. What *present* difference does Christ make? If you obey Christ, what difference will it make this week? The Savior we offer a young person changes our eternity—and our *days*, as well.

The World Doesn't Interest Them

Probably the most uninformed kids in the world—about the world, that is—are American teenagers. Most of them don't know who is in charge of what country. They don't know where any country is. They don't know what's going on politically, and they couldn't care less. They only really care about the small world of who's going with whom and what's going on Friday night and when's the next concert.

Most teenagers do not like to watch the news. They are not interested in reading the newspaper or knowing much about current events. Young people in many other parts of the world are very aware of what is going on in the world. But not American kids. They're only aware of what's on TV tonight or Chopped Liver's new CD.

A school principal told me, "During the 1960s I had a problem with student unrest in my school. Now, I've got a worse problem . . . student rest." He said, "I can't get them interested in anything."

A youth pastor said, "I've been away from kids for about five years, so I thought I should find out what they're thinking and what the issues are. So I started to hang around the local school to find out." He said, "You know what I found out? They don't have issues. They only care about their music, their friends, their party."

Young people live in a small, often trivial, universe. We have to lift their eyes from their mirrors to a world that desperately needs them. It is critical, especially for our Christian kids, to become interested in that world "God so loved." The only way they will ever get to care about that world is if they touch it. They need to get involved in an urban neighborhood, get to know and help some homeless people, visit a rescue mission or a nursing home, or tutor some inner-city kids. "Small world" kids should travel to Mexico, Haiti, South America, or a Native American Indian reservation on a "make a difference" mission. Since they are experience-oriented people, until that world happens to them they will never care about it.

After the world comes alive in their hands, they will never forget it. They care about the world that's happening to them, not the world that's "out there." Effective youth leaders bring the world "out there" right down to their hearts.

Commitment Is Too Risky

Usually it is hard to get kids even to make a commitment for Friday night. "Are you coming Friday night?" Mumbling. "What did you say?" Mumbling—"I'll try. I'll see. I hope so. I might." They won't tell you no and they won't tell you yes.

I remember hearing about a man who was asked, "Do you

have a hard time making decisions?" He said, "Yes and no." That could well have been a contemporary teenager. Their struggle with commitment affects everything from homework to holiness. Young people are reluctant to make long-term commitments to anything.

Why is living together more popular than it has ever been? People think they can have a partner without making a commitment. Why is the age of marriage getting later in life? One reason is that many young men have a Peter Pan problem. They don't want to grow up, and they have a commitment phobia. They get to the edge of the commitment cliff and say, "I really love you, but if that means I'll have to make a commitment to you, bye-bye."

This generation thinks commitment is too risky. Their attitude is: "I want to wait and see if something better comes along." In case it does, they don't want to be locked into one thing . . . whether it's a Friday night event or wedding vows.

Before many young people will make a commitment to Christ, they must first make a commitment to *commitment*. We must show them that commitment leads ultimately to freedom, not limitation . . . to a bigger world, not a smaller one.

Sex Is Expected . . . and Confusing

In the superficial world of the young, sex is equated with love. Today many, many kids feel that if they have sex, they'll have love. Unfortunately, the reality is more like a single person wearing a wedding ring, assuming it will make him or her married. But the ring is only a *symbol* of being married, just as sex is a symbol, an expression of lifetime love.

When young people have sex without a lifetime commitment, they are grabbing the symbol and thinking, "I got the ring. How come I don't have a marriage?" Kids get the symbol, but they don't get the substance, so they ask, "Why am I so lonely?" They went to the love vending machine, paid the price, and got nothing back.

Survey results vary, but averaging them shows us that between 70 and 80 percent of American teenagers have had sex by the end of high school. The tragedy is not only that most teenagers have sex, but that it is *expected* they will. Media images don't help: Commercials exploit sex; prime-time television shows assume that dating includes sex. Nowadays, instead of a girl apologizing because she isn't a virgin, she has to apologize because she is. "You mean you haven't done it yet? What's wrong with you?" The pressure to be sexually active is intense.

One unsettling change is related to who is doing the talking about sexual experiences. It used to be just *guys* in the locker room talking about what they had done and with whom. Now the girls are doing as much talking as the guys are. Today, even the young women are talking about guys' anatomy, their sexual conquests and experiences.

In describing the spiritual decline of the human race, the Bible talks about the ultimate moral collapse. It says, "Even their women exchanged natural relations for unnatural ones" (Romans 1:26). Why does it say, *"Even the women"*? Because when the women are gone, the society's gone. They are the last line of decency.

It is happening at younger and younger ages. Research shows that two out of five kids have had sex *before they are out of junior high.*[2]

It's nice to sit back and think, "What a relief, I'm glad our kids are in youth group. I'm glad they know better." Alarmingly, Josh McDowell's research on church teenagers revealed that by the age of eighteen, 43 percent of the conservative youth group kids have had sex.[3] According to the statistics, by the time they're out of high school, almost half of the youth group have had sex. Other survey answers show that 66 percent have done everything but had sex. They're just technical virgins.

The good news is that many young people, Christian and non-Christian, are open to some authoritative answers about sex. They know their relationships are superficial and that they haven't found love this way. They are tired of "l-o-v-e" ending up being spelled "u-s-e-d."

Sometimes I say to kids, "If you had a system, a machine in a factory, and *half* of the things that it made broke, would you get a new machine? Would you say there's something wrong with that machine?" Half of the lifetime relationships produced by this dating and mating system break! A thinking young person can see that it is time to scrap our sex-driven "relationship machine" for something that produces lasting love.

That leads us to a radical proposal for a culture where sex is out of control. Ask the kids, "Why don't we find out who invented sex and ask Him how it works best?" The Bible reveals the Inventor's identity—"God 'made them male and female' . . . the two will become one flesh" (Mark 10:6, 8). *God* invented it all. Following the Inventor's guidelines will lead a young person to the best of love.

If teenagers see that you are coming to them with a proposal of sexual morality because you care about their love and their future, and not just because you have a rulebook they should live by, they will listen to you. You come to them lovingly, saying, "I want the best for you. God wants the best for you. And here's the road to it." You will find a receptive audience, because they know "love nineties-style" isn't working. There is too much loneliness, too much disease, too much disappointment. They are more ready for sexual answers than perhaps ever before.

These Teenagers Are Post-Christian

Today, we are living in America's first post-Christian generation. Before this generation, most people at least knew what morality was, knew the basic outlines of the Gospel, and had heard John 3:16. Today, that is no longer true. As *Christianity Today* pointed out, Christians in America no longer have the home-field advantage. We are the visiting team. The United States is now "the greatest mission field in the Western hemisphere."[4]

I heard Dr. Jay Kesler make this perceptive observation: We have grandparents who had a Christian belief, parents who have a memory of that belief, and now kids who have nothing. They are spiritually and biblically illiterate. Lost kids today do not know the most basic Bible stories or names. We must assume nothing about their biblical knowledge. If they hear a story about the life of Jesus, for example, they may well be hearing it for the first time.

Martin Marty, the church historian from the University of Chicago, said in a front-page article on evangelicals in the *Wall Street Journal*, "If you're part of the evangelical sub-culture . . . you go to church, you buy the religious books, you watch the television programs. But if you're not part of the sub-culture, you never know it exists."[5] There is a total disconnection between the world of God's people and the world of lost people. God's people know little or nothing about where lost people are today, and lost people seem to not even know that God's people exist.

So those of us who are concerned about teenagers find ourselves in the middle of the *most unreached generation* in the history of North America. Because they are a blank slate spiritually, today's teenagers are easily deceived by the devil's lies. They're ready for anything that feels religious or spiritual because they have no truth by which to measure it. This post-Christian teenager is extremely vulnerable.

But he is also amazingly reachable with the Good News of

Jesus Christ. A contemporary young person probably carries less religious baggage than any previous generation. You can get right to the real issue—Jesus. A teenager today is ready for Jesus. Unfortunately, since he's ready for *anything* spiritual, it all depends on who gets there first.

THE COMPELLING BOTTOM LINE

There is a bottom line that has driven me for more than thirty years in ministry. At least three-fourths of all those who ever accept Jesus Christ do so by the age of eighteen.[6] When you go to the local high school graduation and watch the kids walking across that platform, realize that those who don't know Christ then will probably live and die and spend eternity without Him. *The church of Jesus Christ has nothing more urgent to do than reach people before their lives turn hard—while they are young.* What more important, more urgent mission do we have? We must work "as long as it is day." For sooner than ever, "night is coming, when no one can work" (John 9:4)

The battle rages for a generation of young people. They live all around your neighborhood, your church, even in your own home. You drive by them all the time. They are very lonely, very wounded, very lost. Hope for them begins when a heart for them emerges in some caring Christian adult. Maybe you. Maybe your church.

We have tried to look inside their hearts to see who they really are. We stand at the end of a bridge, looking across at young people who desperately need to know and live for Jesus. If God has begun to break your heart for them, then you are ready to start taking the steps that will bring you into their lives.

1. *Newsweek*, 1975.

2. Karen Levey, "Teens' Sex Levels Still High," *The [Northern New Jersey] Record*, 8 December 1992.

3. "Study Shows Church Kids Are Not Waiting," *Christianity Today*, 18 March 1988, 54–55.

4. George G. Hunter III, "Can the West Be Won?" *Christianity Today*, 16 December 1991, 43.

5. Martin Marty, "Old Time Religion," *Wall Street Journal*, front page, 11 July 1980.

6. George Barna, *Generation Next* (Venture, Calif: Regal, 1996), 77.

3

How to Rescue Lost Young People: The Imperatives

osnia. A place few Americans had ever heard of suddenly dominated the evening news night after night. Then in December 1995, thousands of U.S. troops were poised to enter this country which few Americans could locate on a map. The mission was to assist the United Nations peacekeeping force in securing stability in that war-ravaged land. But for most of those American soldiers, the mission looked like Mission Impossible—because of a river.

The first major battle in the Bosnian mission was finding a way to get into Bosnia.

The Sava River stood between thousands of troops coming from the north and their mission. It was winter . . . the river was flooding . . . and it was a long way across. But in an impressive display of military engineering and cooperation, the bridge across the Sava—longer than the Brooklyn Bridge—was built. The forces who had come to make a difference were able to cross that bridge to accomplish their mission.

As we explore the heart condition of modern young people without Jesus, we, in essence, are looking at them from one bank of a broad river. On our side of the river are the men and women "whose hearts God [has] touched" (1 Samuel 10:26) with the lostness of those kids. The challenge is this: The young people who need us are on the other side of a great divide. Teenagers today know almost nothing about the world of Christians—and Christians know almost nothing about the world of teenagers. They have never been farther apart.

So Christian adults who want to make a difference for lost kids must figure out *how to build a bridge into the lives they have been called to rescue*. These are post-Christian kids—"loster" than kids have ever been in our part of the world. In fact, their pain, self-destructiveness, and spiritual ignorance could discourage a caring adult.

Culturally, language-wise, they are far from the world of the church. So those of us who want to bring them Jesus will have to do what Jesus did—"seek and save" those who are lost (Luke 19:10). It will require daring and ingenuity—like the building of a bridge across the Sava River. But without the bridge into lost teenagers' lives, the hope will never reach them.

The mission bridge is made up of five life-saving imperatives. Any adult who hopes to enter young lives with the Good News of Jesus will commit himself or herself to the steps defined by these imperatives.

FOCUS ON JESUS

Teenagers are not interested in hearing about religion, denomination, or lifestyle issues. It is the *person of Jesus* that will interest a modern young person, not the system of Christianity.

Our family has taken a son and a daughter to college. Taking a girl is more traumatic, because apparently a girl is much more attached to all the little things in her world. She has to take her whole world to college with her. When Lisa headed for college, she had ten jammed suitcases and two trunks. It was difficult to get anywhere with that much baggage. After my oldest son finished moving his sister into her dorm, he said, "When I go to college, I'm taking a toothbrush, a Bible, and underwear. That's it."

If you are trying to move into a lost teenager's life with a lot of theological and religious baggage, you may not be able to get anywhere. One of the greatest theologians of all time, the apostle Paul, says in 1 Corinthians 2:2, "I resolved to know nothing while I was with you except *Jesus Christ and him crucified*" (italics added). Paul could have come to Corinth with a ton of Christian truth, but instead he focused on a simple message . . . Jesus and the Cross.

There certainly is an appropriate time to teach the whole counsel of God, but it is probably not when you are trying to introduce a post-Christian teenager to the basics of the Gospel. It is important to address lifestyle issues, as well—a young person's language, music, and relationships. But there is no point in trying to get teenagers to try to clean up before they know the Cleaner-Upper. Our focus needs to be on a Person—just show them Jesus and His love displayed on that cross. They need to hear an unencumbered Gospel.

When dealing with teenagers today, it is helpful to use the Gospels (Matthew, Mark, Luke, and John) extensively. They need to hear the stories of Jesus and find out how He treats people, what He expects of people, what His love and power are like. For example, the story of the Samaritan woman (John 4) shows how Jesus works in the life of someone who has been looking for love in all the wrong places—like so many teenagers. The story of Zacchaeus (Luke 19) tells what happens when someone who has always felt little meets Jesus—he becomes a truly big man for the first time in his life.

Young people love stories, and some of the best stories in all the world are the ones right out of the Gospels. Teenagers begin to "meet" Jesus when we figure out ways to enter into those stories. Who is Bartimaeus? He's an outsider. He's the fellow who's yelling for attention, "Hello, I'm over here." Finally when Jesus comes, he says, "Jesus, please notice me." This is something a lot of young people can relate to. Walk around in Bible stories, try to feel the feelings of people, and look for points of identification for teenagers.

It is instructive that Jesus often extended a simple invitation to people—*"Follow Me."* Following Jesus is the bottom line. Jesus says, "It's you and Me. What are you going to do with Me? I'm extending a hand to you. Are you going to follow Me or stay where you are?" This is a one-on-one thing. I am grateful that Jesus doesn't say, "Follow My leaders or My TV evangelists." Jesus never said "Follow My followers." Some people say, "My grandmother and the people in my church are hypocrites." Well, the Bible does not say, "Follow your grandmother." Was Jesus a hypocrite? "What about the nun who hit me when I was five and made me follow all those rules?" Did Jesus say, "Follow the nun" or "Follow the rules"? No, Jesus said, "Follow Me." Unless someone has a problem with Jesus, there is no other reason to reject Him. Jesus made Himself the issue. So tell the story of Jesus.

This Jesus-focus will keep us from non-Gospel detours such

as Adam and Eve, inconsistencies in the church, or music. We simply must lead them and keep them on the shortest possible road to Jesus and His Cross. If the conversation starts to stray from the Gospel Road, we must keep bringing the conversation back to Jesus. "Yes, but what about *Jesus* and what He did for you on the cross?"

For many years, I ran a Campus Life club in our town in northern New Jersey. I would occasionally stand back and think about who these kids were, listening to my Gospel wrap-ups—they were Catholic, Protestant, Jewish, Muslim, Hindu, and nothing. Lots of lost kids. I remember one planning meeting our club staff had where our volunteers were expressing some of their concerns—rowdiness during the crowdbreakers, occasional failure to listen to each other's comments during the group discussion, and scattered talking sometimes during my wrap-up.

Then one volunteer made a revealing observation—"They don't always quiet down when you're talking about a teenage issue, or even about God. But as soon as you mention Jesus, it is suddenly totally quiet in the room." Everyone agreed.

That has been my consistent experience, in large audiences and small. No matter how restless the crowd may be, an amazing hush stills those young people as soon as I present Jesus and His Cross. "Kings and kingdoms will all pass away, but there is *still* something about that Name!"

Focus on Jesus. He is everything a young heart is hungry for.

START WITH THEIR NEED

The second imperative for adults building a bridge to lost young people deals with your *starting point* in presenting Jesus. Initially, a young person does not care much about Jesus or an answer to sin—that would be *our* starting point. So we need to begin with a need that young person *does* care about. This sensitivity in evangelism was modeled by Jesus Himself in His conversation with the Samaritan woman (John 4).

Notice that Jesus doesn't walk up and say, "Hi, I'm the Messiah." Instead He says, "Hi. Let's talk water" (a loose translation). Jesus had almost nothing in common with this lady. He was a man, she was a woman. He was a Jew, she was a Samaritan. He was a Rabbi, she was a promiscuous woman. Yet Jesus found something in common to talk about: Their mutual need was water. So Jesus started talking about physical thirst; then He moved to emotional and spiritual thirst and the living water He offered.

Emulating the Jesus-model, we should start with a teenager on the level of his or her felt needs. The first point in your Gospel-sharing outline should be the person you are talking with. A young person is thinking, *Why should I care about what you're trying to tell me? What does it have to do with my life?* Remembering that teenagers are feeling-focused, now-oriented people, we can best introduce them to Jesus if we *start with their need.*

Sin-Scarred Lives

Unfortunately, sin is a non-issue to today's kids. Playing on a field where they see no boundaries, they feel no sin problem. And since sin is a non-issue, a Savior is also a non-issue. What difference does it make if "Jesus died for our sin" when I don't even know that sin is a problem? So "How do you present the Gospel to kids like these?" is an important question.

Sin is not an issue to today's lost kids, but the *results* of sin are very much an issue. They are experts on the results of sin, but they do not know that sin is what causes those results. They can see what selfishness is doing to their family and their parents' marriage . . . the scars left on people by rampant verbal cruelty . . . the emotional scars left on them and their peers by sexual using, disguised as love. They see the brokenness all around them, the superficiality in their relationships, the incurable loneliness. And young people know all too well what one young woman described to me as "the darkness inside of me that scares me"—the anger, the pain, the depression.

In other words, young people may not know about the *disease,* but they see the *symptoms* all around them and inside of them. We can lead them from where they are to the cross of Jesus if we begin with the symptoms of sins they can see . . . show them the sin-disease that causes that symptom . . . then introduce to them the *cure* provided by Jesus Christ. It is like going from the symptom to the cancer to the cure. Start with the disease—little interest. Start with the symptom—they're listening.

Symptom—Disease—Cure

There is a danger in starting with their starting point. It is all too easy to skip from the symptom to the cure without ever explaining the disease of sin. Loneliness would be an example of a sin-symptom kids are very much aware of—and an effective place to begin. But Jesus did not die for loneliness. He died for sin.

But ultimately, loneliness, as Billy Graham has said, is cosmic loneliness. No earth-person can fill the hole in our hearts because God has "set eternity in the hearts of men" (Ecclesiastes 3:11). It's *God* we are ultimately lonely for, because we are away from the One who created us. We are away from Him because of this un-God way of living called sin. Until the sin-disease is somehow dealt with, the symptom of loneliness cannot go away. And that realization brings a young person to the Cross, where our sin-disease is borne by the Son of God. We cannot present the Gospel if we leave out sin.

Whenever we present Christ to lost young people, it is important to follow this symptom/disease/cure approach. One example would be the night I told a group of kids that I would give an award for the three best put-downs. Normally I would not give an award, since this is not behavior I want to encourage. But I said, "Come up front, and without directing it to anybody in the room, give us your three best put-downs." After the contest, I said, "Do any of you wonder why we are so good at put-downs? How many of you have ever been put down? How many of you have ever been called a name you can still remember and it hurt?"

Then I discussed how this tongue of ours seems out of control. "What would happen if everybody bled physically every time they were cut emotionally or verbally?" I said, "They would need to hire twenty more custodians in the school to mop up blood, because of how many times kids are cut verbally every day. Since we know it hurts people, why do we do this?"

I asked, "Have you ever felt like there's this animal inside of you that keeps doing things that you don't want to do and that you're not proud of when you're done? You ask yourself, 'Why do I hurt the people I love most? I know I don't like it. The people around me don't like it. I suppose God doesn't like it. The people who love me the most are the people I've done the most damage to. What is wrong with me?'

"Well, there is an animal inside all of us. Everybody has felt at sometime, 'I don't want to cut people down. I would like to build people up. I'd like for people to feel big after they're around me, not little, but what's my problem?'

"Two thousand years ago Jesus Christ named the animal. He put it this way, 'Everyone who sins is a slave to sin' (John 8:34). Jesus said, 'There is this animal named sin.' There is this dark force and dark energy inside of us that leads to the dark decisions that we make. The dark power inside of us and the dark side of us continues to make wrong choices and do things we wish we wouldn't do. If you could tame the animal, you would have by now, because you don't like it.

"Good News. Not only did Jesus name the animal, but He tamed the animal. John 8:36 says, 'If the Son sets you free, you will be free indeed.' Free from the animal inside. How could He do that? Because the day He died, He turned all of the fury of the animal on Himself and said, 'Take Me so you don't ever have to take them.'"

There was more to this talk, of course, but this summary illustrates communication that brings teenagers from where *they* are to where *Jesus* is. What we say will matter to them if we address something that already matters to them.

A Relational Savior

What matters most to kids today? Relationships. Therefore, what kinds of sin-symptoms will they see the most? Symptoms that affect relationships—symptoms such as selfishness, jealousy, prejudice, pregnancy, anger, verbal cruelty, lack of commitment, divorce, sexual scars. They can see the damage sin is doing to the thing they care the most about . . . relationships. So that is a sensitive place to start. That's like going to the well and talking about water with the woman of Samaria. That's where they live. That's what they drink from. They drink from relationships. And something has poisoned their well. Most kids know the well has been poisoned, but they do not know what the poison is.

If you want to begin with their need, you could say to almost any teenager today, "Have you ever felt like there is someone missing in your life . . . like there's someone who's supposed to be there but isn't?" Even the young person who is riding the top of the wave, and is the president and captain of everything, still feels like something's missing. Kids are feeling the "missingness" of God, but they do not know that is what's missing. They experience it in a dozen different ways. In their loneliness, they're lonely for God. They feel despair, hopelessness, and meaninglessness that comes from their distance from God. The One who knows why they're here, they can't get to. Whether it's a fear of life or a fear of death, the problem goes back to the "missingness" of God.

The first imperative of focusing on Jesus and the second

imperative of starting with their need come together when we share the Gospel as a *relationship*—life's most important relationship. This message we tell is about a Person, not a religion. We connect with their need on the level of this Ultimate Relationship. Chapter 6 will look closer at how to do this.

PACKAGE IT ATTRACTIVELY

Companies spend millions to develop a package in which to sell you their product—design, slogan, jingle, ad campaign, etc. They know something we as Christians sometimes forget—even a superior product may not sell if it is presented in an uninteresting package.

Why is it that so many young people are buying what Satan is selling? His product is ultimately only darkness and death. But the enemy has some of the most attractive *packages* in the world. Why is it so many young people are ignoring the love and life that Jesus offers? Could it be because we are presenting that incredible "product" in some terribly *boring* packages? Too often we expect a teenager to be attracted to Christ through approaches that he or she probably considers irrelevant, uninteresting, and culturally foreign. Then we interpret his disinterest as rejection of Christ when, in reality, he may be rejecting the package in which we have presented Him.

The great cross-cultural missionary Paul understood and lived the packaging principle. In describing his evangelism approach, he says, "To the Jews I became like a Jew." In other words, he put the Gospel in a Jewish package to win the Jews. "To those under the law I became like one under the law"—he put it in an "under-the-law" package. Then "to those not having the law, I became like one not having the law"—yes, a "not-having-the-law" wrapper. And finally, "To the weak I became weak, to win the weak." His bottom line: "I have become all things to all men so that by all possible means I might save some. I do all this for the sake of the gospel" (1 Corinthians 9:20–23). "By all possible means" . . . what a description of youth ministry! Did Paul care about the package? Obviously. Did he ever change the product, the message? Never!

Effective cross-cultural ministry—reaching youth culture "natives"—brings a never-changing message in an ever-relevant package. The problem with much of our youth-outreach approach is that Christian programs are almost always planned *by* the already interested *for* the already interested. If you already care about Christian things, you might like this program. But whenever we are planning an outreach for young people, we have to think *sixteen and lost*—not thirty-five and found!

It is important to look at our methods through "sixteen and lost" eyes. If I were sixteen and lost, would I come to this? Would I understand it? Would I feel at home in this setting? Would I come back?

Practically speaking, what are some of the ingredients in a package that will reach today's young person? We will go into those ingredients in a future chapter. For now, we simply need to understand the imperative of an attractive package for our life-giving message.

The tragedy would be having the only Answer for a lost teenager and having him walk right by that Answer because of our unappealing package. For many teenagers, Jesus is only a name they hear profaned all day long at school. They must have a chance to hear who He really is.

Yes, there is a whole world of Christian radio, Christian TV, Christian publications, Christian meetings, Christian music, and Christian concerts out there—but most lost kids don't even know that world exists. The Jesus-orbit is another universe to them. It is up to us to give them a reason to come to a Jesus-place.

GO TO THEIR WORLD

The fourth life-saving imperative calls us to leave our comfort zone and go to the places where lost kids are. We cannot keep waiting for them to come to us. Again, we are asked to copy the Master's model for reaching us. The Bible does not say, "The word became flesh and called a meeting and invited us to come." No, it tells us, "The word became flesh and *made His dwelling among us*" (John 1:14, italics added). The original Greek words suggest something like "He pitched His tent next to ours."

Jesus did not go to the synagogue and say, "Saturday night we are having a big rally, so everyone come and hear what I have to say." Yes, He had some public meetings, many of which seemed to spring up spontaneously, such as the Sermon on the Mount. It is still important to have meetings, and we still need to have outreaches. But the point is that the real ministry of Jesus was on the dock, at the wedding, at the party, at the dinner, on the street. This is a God who comes to where we are, not one who asks us to come where He is.

We need to reach kids the way Jesus reached people. We need to go where they are. Some people think, "I'd be scared to death to go where they are. I don't know if I'd feel real comfortable." Frankly, one of the hardest parts of youth ministry for me has been showing up on a campus or at a school activity. It's tough to go to a high school and say, "Hi, kids—let's meet." Do I want to go there? Do I want to go to a game? Do I want to be at a practice? Is that what I want to do as a man my age? No. Is it safe for me? Do I feel real comfortable? No.

But is it what my Savior did? Yes. Did He come among us because it was the comfortable thing to do? Do I think He'd enjoy coming here and living in this ghetto to reach me? Do I think He loved all the parties and banquets He went to? No. But Jesus took those risks, knowing I would never come to Him and that He would have to come to me. Incarnational evangelism goes where the people are. And incarnational evangelism is what our Savior taught us by His model. That's why reaching people means leaving the safety of the life-saving station where I'd like to spend my whole life, going to life-saving seminars and singing life-saving songs while not one life is rescued. I have to get out in the surf and risk the storm. A person has to take risks to reach people. There is no evangelism without risk. Ask Jesus.

A caring adult who is going to reach kids is going to find a way to take the Gospel to kids' places or find other people on their team who can. You may or may not be the person who will do it, but you could train, teach, prepare, or motivate others to do it.

Incarnational Evangelism

A little boy repeatedly told his mother, "Mommy, I'm having a hard time getting to sleep."

She'd say, "Well, remember, honey, God is in the room with you. Good night." She'd leave and five minutes later hear, "Mommy." Finally, after her fourth return visit, the mother said, "Honey, I've told you, God is in this room with you even when I'm not."

The little boy answered with childlike candor, "Mommy, I just wish God had some skin on."

That's how teenagers feel. "I wish God had some skin on." Fortunately, He does. That's why Jesus came . . . God with skin on.

For God to have skin on for these kids, we who are His ambassadors are going to have to go into a teenager's world. What are some ways for a caring adult to meet kids in their world? Here are some ideas.

Most communities have a youth center of some kind, and usually these places are looking for volunteers. They never have enough people to help run and chaperone their activities. We ought to be sending in an army of Christians to volunteer at the youth center. Some of Jesus' representatives should be running the basketball league; being a coach, a chaperone, or a supervisor; sweeping the floors—just to be where the kids are.

Some people do substitute teaching every once in awhile to be in touch with local teenagers. If you have the credentials, you might offer yourself as a substitute teacher in a school that is in your community or one that you want to affect. Be the best, most caring, most loving substitute they ever had. If you remember some of the substitute teachers you had, you know it would not take much to stand out as one who actually cared about the kids, instead of passing through their lives and picking up a check.

Another effective way to meet young people in their world is to be at a school sporting event, especially if you know somebody who is going to be in a game. A natural way to meet kids is to be at their game or at their practice and have one teenager introduce you to another. If you know one teenager, you can meet some more—if you go to where those friends are. One caution is to avoid embarrassing a young person by being too forward. To meet them, quietly say, if you're with the teenager that you know, "My name's Ron. I don't think I've met you before." That can be followed up with a question about what grade they are in or how they happen to know the teenager you're with.

The point is that you can have one teenager lead you to another. For example, if you go to a soccer match alone, people may wonder who you are and if you're selling drugs or something. It is best if you go with someone who could introduce you to people. Going to a game or a practice or an activity will mean much to the kids you know because you're showing up at *their* thing. If their interest is something you don't know much about, then let them teach you about it. A great way to build a relationship is to say, "Frankly I don't know a whole lot about this sport or about cars or about this activity—how does this work?" You may think you sound pretty "uncool," but you are actually giving that teenager a chance to teach this big adult something. That has a great chance of endearing you to the one you let be "smarter" than you.

Service Evangelism

Another great way to go to their world is to be of service to school organizations. Sometimes we only try to get kids to come to our organization. We set up this little group over on the side, and say, "You all come to our group over here." Well, some of them are already in a group—so why don't we see if we can find a way to attach ourselves to what they're already in?

I remember the day our local high school marching band was out in the hot days of August practicing their football half-time routine. So I called some ladies and asked, "How would you like to do some evangelistic baking? I'll explain later, but could you bake some chocolate chip cookies?"

After clearing it with the band director, we showed up on the field about three o'clock in the afternoon. We set up some folding tables covered with goodies. As the kids came up to get lemonade and cookies they were asking, "Who are you people? Where are you from?" It was nice to say, "Well, we're from Campus Life and we thought you could use a little lift today." Many of them already knew me, but that brought us right into their world. That day serving chocolate chip cookies and lemonade was the equivalent of washing feet for a hot, tired band member (I much prefer cookies over feet).

When you apply the concept of servanthood to school organizations, you can end up right in the middle of lost young people. Could you chaperone a trip or an activity? Chaperones are hard to find. Is there something you can do for the chorus, for the band, for the football team, for the soccer team, for the girls' basketball team, for the computer club? Could you take pictures for them? Could you drive for them?

Some people drive a school bus a morning or two a week just to meet kids. Many school bus drivers act like they are a part of the machine. But if you care and you learn a few names and express some interest, you are making natural contact with them. If you are interested in "seeking and saving those who are lost," you will find your own personal way to get involved in a teenager's world. There are dozens of ways to do it. But you've got to go to their places.

If you can shoot baskets, kick a soccer ball, throw a football, or hit a baseball, go out with a "ball in one hand and a Bible in the other" (figuratively) and meet some young people. Or you can meet young people through "research" about teenagers at local malls or hang-outs. If possible, go with a tape recorder or a video camera. You can explain, "I'm doing research on the youth culture to help explain teenagers' feelings to adults. Could I ask you a few questions?" That can be followed with questions about subjects such as "the problem with relationships," "one of our greatest fears about the future," or "one thing I wish parents understood about us." That's a quick way to meet kids.

A camera or a video camera opens up new opportunities to broaden your youth contacts. For example, I had a wonderful opportunity in recent years in a public high school to lead a pre-football game "meeting" each week for the players. It was called "the meeting," and each week the coach gave me some subject to deal with that related to sports. We took a story out of the Bible, maybe David and Goliath, Joshua and Jericho, or Jesus in the storm, then presented some biblical principles. At the end of the season, our Campus Life group raised money for a dinner for all the football players, where we had a Christian professional football player come and share his testimony. I would give an invitation and every year ten to fifteen of the players gave their lives to Christ.

How did this kind of rare opportunity arise? It started with a camera. There is one thing every athlete loves—a picture of himself or herself in action. So if you get a good picture of an athlete in action, that athlete will probably like you. He or she will want to know who you are and where you are showing the pictures. I went to practices and games with my trusty slide camera. I asked the coach if he would be interested in some of those slides—he sure was. Eventually, even the principal would call and ask for the slides. They were used at pep rallies and the annual parents' booster banquet. From that simple connection, a relationship developed with the coaches and the team that led to those pre-game get-togethers.

So, get a camera and see what develops. When teenagers ask where you are showing what you shot, you can tell them about your big hamburger or pizza party with them appearing on the big screen.

These few examples are only a sampling of the ways a Jesus-ambassador can enter the world of unreached young people. Ultimately, it all starts in the heart when you allow Jesus to give you

His shepherd's heart—the kind that pursues lost sheep instead of waiting for them to come to you.

If our Master were to come today and do youth ministry, you would find Him at the school . . . at the game . . . at the places kids hang out. He would seek them out.

In rescuing dying young people, the easy way—planning a meeting and hoping they will come—probably won't rescue many. But if you've gone to their world, they are a lot more likely to come to yours. Even if they never do, you can show them Jesus, meeting or not.

You are like your Master when you take the risks of leaving your safe place to be where the dying people are. A lifeguard doesn't do his work in a life-saving station. He does it out in the storm and the surf.

GIVE THEM LOVE

Four of the five life-saving imperatives for youth evangelism are about what you *do*—present a message focused on Jesus; start with their need; package it attractively; and make contact with kids in their world. The last imperative—in a sense, the bottom line requirement for entering young lives—is about who you *are*. It is about being the kind of person who makes a young person *feel important*.

Some people feel inadequate to work with young people because they aren't "cool" . . . or funny . . . or creative . . . or even outgoing. Others think they may be too old to impact a young person's life. But all of these concerns miss the most fundamental skill of reaching teenagers—the ability to *give them love*. Ultimately, a young person goes where he or she feels loved. And that has nothing to do with how cool or creative or outgoing you are—or how old you are. This has nothing to do with birthdays. There are seventy-year-old people who know how to make a teenager feel loved and twenty-five-year-old people who don't.

If you have the ability to make young people feel important, you can play a vital role in youth ministry. You make them feel important by focusing on them while they are with you, making each person feel like the only person on earth. Teenagers are starved for that kind of focused attention and caring. Many, if not most, do not get it at home. Everyone at school is too self-occupied to love like that. So the adult who provides that kind of quality attention can open a teenager's heart.

You give them love when you listen to them without distraction . . . when you remember to ask about the things that are important in their lives . . . when you go the extra mile to spend time with them . . . when you make a big deal of their big days . . . when you are there for their important times.

The exciting discovery is that this bottom line imperative of youth ministry is something *anyone* can do. It requires no special skill, just a caring heart. Not everyone can preach to young people or entertain them or create activities for them—but anyone can show them love.

No program can do that. In fact, if kids know you love them, you could probably read out of the telephone book at your meeting and they would say, "Hey, that's my friend up there!" While that is not a recommended idea from the "Top Ten Youth Programs," your *relationship* with a young person far outweighs your *program* in importance.

Real love is so hard to come by in a young person's world today that they almost cannot believe you care. But if they consistently feel valued and loved when they are with you, they will ultimately trust you with their heart . . . and maybe one day trust your Savior. In a sense, whoever makes them feel loved first will have their life. I pray it will be a friend of Jesus. Maybe you.

4

How to Rescue Lost Young People: The Weapons

Saddam Hussein never stood a chance. He crowed that his showdown with the Allied Forces would be "the mother of all battles." But the Persian Gulf War was more like the mother of all routs instead. One main reason the battle was won so decisively was the incredible weapons America unleashed on their foes. We spectators sat before our TVs in awe as we watched the dazzling performance of everything from Patriot anti-SCUD missiles to "smart" Tomahawk missiles. In many ways, it all came down to who had the superior weapons.

It is the same in the battle for a generation of young people in your community. If having the superior *cause* were enough, then the Gospel should be capturing large numbers of young hearts. But if you spent a day in a local high school or junior high, you would almost surely conclude that the darkness is winning, not the Light.

In order to win the battle, the people with the superior Cause must fight with the winning *weapons*. We must never forget that this is *war*.

It is life-or-death; we are contesting with the Prince of Darkness himself for the lives of kids in our area, and we must fight with the intensity of warriors. Youth ministry is ultimately not about eating pizza, playing basketball, and leading activities—it is fierce spiritual combat that calls for serious commitment.

The winning weapons in this battle are not youth meetings, activities, and programs. They are spiritual weapons that are energized by the power of God. And these weapons are modeled in flesh and blood in one of the most practical and challenging books of the Bible—the book of Nehemiah.

Nehemiah is a textbook for people who have a big job, a short time, and a few people. In this amazing chapter of Jewish history, a relatively small group of people have to rebuild the walls and gates of the city of Jerusalem—and they get it done in fifty-two days.

Reaching a generation of kids in your town is definitely a Nehemiah Project. You have an overwhelming task and only a few people who care about lost young people. In addition, time is short. So, Nehemiah is for us: Few people. Big job. Short time. They were building a city; we are building young lives. But the weapons that won Nehemiah's battle are the same ones that will win ours. Nehemiah's "battle journal" arms us with five weapons that will win the battle for young lives.

INCURABLE HEART TROUBLE

The first winning weapon is found in Nehemiah 1:4. Earlier in the chapter Nehemiah received a report that the holy city of Jerusalem was a disaster. Its gates had been burned with fire and its walls had fallen, so now anything could get into the city of Jerusalem. The city that Nehemiah loved had no protection. What a description of young people today! Anything can get into their lives. The walls that once protected them in the turbulence of growing up—family, faith, future expectancy—have been devalued or destroyed. Now anything can get in—and almost everything is.

Here is Nehemiah's reaction: "When I heard these things, I sat down and called a committee meeting." No. "I sat down and planned a program." No again. In his book he says, *I sat down and wept.*" Other people knew about this need. The men who brought back the report from Jerusalem reported factually, "Jerusalem is a mess." But for Nehemiah the need of his city was something deeply moving, deeply disturbing. It broke his heart.

And that is the first winning weapon in the battle for young people—*a broken heart.*

Nehemiah seems an unlikely candidate to be the answer to the problem of Jerusalem. First of all, he was not even there. He was in another world, apparently in no position to make a difference. That is how some people feel about rescuing young people— "I'm not very close to the world of teenagers . . . what could I do?" Nehemiah was a cupbearer to the king. He was not in construction or carpentry. It doesn't seem like he had the right qualifications or the right location. And, yet, God used him to change the course of history. Where did it start? Nehemiah had no idea he was going to end up leading the reconstruction of the city of Jerusalem and being the governor. All Nehemiah knew was that he had a broken heart, and the need moved him to tears.

Who would guess that such a crusade could begin with one man, crying in his room, connected to the need only by his heart? But that is always where major spiritual breakthroughs begin— with one broken heart. There may be people more trained, more gifted, but you are the one whose heart God has broken. That is the number-one qualification for a person to make a difference.

Heart trouble is serious business in our family, especially with my father's cardiac history. But more than thirty years ago, God gave me another kind of heart trouble—and it is incurable. I pray you may have it too. It is a heart that is broken over teenage lostness.

You know you have it if something happens in your heart when you see kids wandering a mall, hoping that something or someone will happen to them. Or when you see all those teenagers pouring out of the local school, looking like "sheep without a shepherd." Maybe you feel it when you read in the local newspaper about teenage pregnancy or a teenage suicide. Or when you see kids hitchhiking or just hanging out. If you have Jesus-eyes, you see lostness . . . loneliness . . . pain. You see dying people. And your heart aches. Surely the Jesus who wept over His generation must weep over these kids. He wants to place His heart in yours.

That broken heart drives you to keep pursuing more lost young people . . . keeps you going when everyone else is giving up . . . makes you leave your comfort zone and take risks to save lives. This incurable heart trouble makes you an advocate for lost young people in your church. When the church dollars are budgeted, programs are planned, and priorities are set, unreached kids have no voice—unless someone like you is their advocate. They need you to remind your brothers and sisters of the people in town who need them the most.

There is a dangerous prayer that will make you a dangerous person—for the Lord. If you would be a make-a-difference person for the young people in your community, then this will be your prayer—"Go ahead, God . . . break my heart for the kids in this town."

When He answers, you will begin to be armed with a weapon

more powerful than you could ever have imagined. The Nehemiah miracle began with one man in his room, weeping over a need. That is how a miracle will start for the kids where you live.

UNLEASHED POWER

The second winning weapon is also found in Nehemiah 1:4: "For some days I mourned and fasted and prayed before the God of heaven." From a broken heart comes that second weapon—*a desperate prayer crusade.* This prayer vigil apparently lasted for several months before he went to see the king. He regularly, passionately, desperately said, "Oh, God, what are we going to do about this?" In fact, he started out his prayer, "Oh, Lord God of heaven."

I once heard somebody say that one of the ways we will be able to tell that revival is coming in America is when we begin to hear Christians praying, "Oh, God. Oh, Lord." Not, "Dear Lord, bless this meeting. Help this day. Forgive us of our many sins. Help the missionaries, whoever they may be." Nehemiah was a passionate man who modeled desperate, urgent prayer for that which broke his heart. In essence, he said, "Oh, God, Lord of heaven, great and awesome God who keeps His covenant of love, everything I know about You I'm plugging into right now. Lord, only You can do this one and show me what to do."

Spiritual heart trouble takes action—in a consistent, impassioned prayer crusade. For those of us who have a burden for young people, that prayer seeks to focus all the power of heaven on a school, a neighborhood, a people group, a gang, a team, a youth group. At this point, it is not time to plan meetings, create a strategy, or buy a book of a thousand good youth meeting ideas. It's time to *pray*—desperate prayer.

If you decide to make a difference for a world of lost kids around you, you will need His power—and you'll know you need His power. Nehemiah, overwhelmed by this need, said, "I can't do anything but go to the throne room." Nehemiah had access to the most powerful man on earth, the king, in his earthly throne room. But he did not even think about starting there. He went directly to the heavenly throne room and said, "Lord, what do we do about this need?"

The battle for the young people around you must first be won in the heavenlies before it can be won in your youth ministry. Weeks and months of fervent prayer for those kids and for your own life will prepare their hearts and yours. As you pray intensively and extensively out of your broken heart, that third winning weapon will become yours . . .

A DREAM AND A PLAN

After what appears to be several months of praying, a dream and a plan were born in Nehemiah's heart. During Nehemiah's regular duties in the throne room, the king inquired about why his cupbearer was uncharacteristically sad.

Nehemiah basically answered, "My heart is broken over my city." The king responded with a question that must have been planted by the One to whom Nehemiah had been praying—"What is it you want?" "Then I prayed to the God of heaven, and I answered the king," Nehemiah said (2:4–5).

Nehemiah then started listing what he needed: letters, timber, help. Something happened during those times on his knees—he discovered what he later described as "what my God had put in my heart to do" (v. 12). The best plans do not begin in planning meetings; they begin in *prayer* meetings.

As you consider your part in reaching young people, you might well think, "I do not know how we would begin to tackle the kids around our community and around our church." That's fine. That will make you desperately dependent on God. He wants you broken on your knees and needing His power desperately. In that brokenness, He will give you His dream for reaching that school, that neighborhood, that gang, that group of kids. God gives the burden first, then the plan.

Any breakthrough strategy requires both a dream and a plan. A plan without a dream—you won't be motivated enough to do. Or you might say, "We've got to reach these kids." That is an important dream, but without a plan, it will die on the drawing board. Modern Nehemiahs understand that spiritual victories depend on having both the "want to"—the dream—and the "how to"—the plan.

THE EQUIPMENT IN A RESCUE PLAN

An effective plan for reaching unreached young people should include five important pieces of equipment.

Neutral Ground

The first important element is *neutral ground.* If you want to attract lost kids, your meeting place matters. They will be most likely to come to something that is held in a spiritually neutral set-ting—a place where they feel comfortable. We may feel most com-fortable meeting at the church, on *our* ground. But an outreach is not for us. So the location should be something "safe" for lost kids, such as a school, a YMCA, a gym, a park. We must be willing to move out of our safe place in order to reach those who may other-wise never be reached—just as our Savior did.

A Social Hook

The second piece of equipment in our "rescue plan" is *a social hook*. Teenagers need a social reason to come because a spiritual reason probably will not get them there. This approach comes under the New Testament heading of "by all possible means" (1 Corinthians 9:22)—a package that will attract non-Christians to a place where they will hear the Gospel.

Here are some examples of social hooks. *Food.* Teenagers love the idea of an "all-you-can-eat for a couple of bucks" burger cookout, pizza or taco feast, or a world's largest sundae or banana split, where you build the ice cream treat in a rain gutter. Have free or cheap food, and you will have kids.

Secondly, teenagers like activities where they *work together*. Kids in this generation are lonely and detached from each other, so they love to do things that get them involved in projects together. It doesn't necessarily have to be a meaningful thing they are doing—it can be rather dumb even, as long as they are working together. Most teenagers do not know how to facilitate togetherness, so they will enjoy a setting where you make "together" happen.

For example, a video-making night, where you even give awards, like an old sneaker spray-painted gold and mounted as a trophy. Give awards for the best movie, best actor, and so on. The different "movie-making companies" have forty-five minutes to create a video on a subject, film it, and come back for the show-ings. The leader provides a box of props to work from and an over-all theme, such as "superheroes" or "dweeb olympics." It's a crazy project, but they like the feeling of working together in a group.

Right after Thanksgiving it is fun to get a group together to look for the last surviving turkey. Have the turkey waiting in some-body's pickup truck in a parking lot as the teenagers, in teams by vans, follow a series of five clues that take them around town to get it.

The concept of working together can be used on a more serious level by sometimes facilitating small group discussions. Initially, it can be hard to get teenagers talking, but they have a lot to express if you create the right climate. They might not respond if you said to them, "Describe some temptations that you face." But they would be more likely to finish a sentence like this: "One of the biggest temptations teenagers struggle with is . . ." Ask them to say the first thing that comes to their mind. Also, if you want to get kids talking, it is most effective to start with a nonthreatening question first, moving to questions that require more personal answers.

If we were talking about temptation, how would we approach that? Maybe by starting off with a statement to finish like: "When you're seven years old, something that's really tempting is . . ." Answers will be "to hit your little brother" or "to hide your report card." Seven-year-old feelings are not very threatening to talk about. We might move from that to a second question such as, "When you're sixteen, one of life's big temptations is . . ." In this way, you are tapering from the safe and the broad to the more personal and specific. You will also find that teenagers will talk more openly in a small group if you give a personal anecdote first and answer the question you are asking them to answer. If you are vulnerable and answer it yourself, you have shown that it is OK to talk about that subject.

Once you begin to create a comfortable small group dynamic, it will emerge as a reason to come to your meetings. Because young people are looking for connectedness and a safe place to voice their feelings, this kind of "working together" will become an attraction in itself.

A third social hook is *nonthreatening competition*, especially the kind where you do not have to be an athlete to have fun. You do not want to create a program that is only for those who feel confident athletically. Gym nights can be strong drawing cards with volleyball or a variety of games going simultaneously. Another example of a nonthreatening competition is a "world's largest pillow fight." If you have ever seen two kids armed with pillows, you can imagine what happens when you have a hundred kids armed with pillows, fighting it out in a gym in several planned events. A few years ago, one of the groups I was involved with advertised a world's largest pillow fight for our local school. About eighty-five kids came—and eighteen of them gave their lives to Christ that night! They came because of a social hook—mugging each other with pillows. By the time they heard the music and testimony of a Christian band and a short Gospel wrap-up, many of them left with Christ in their hearts.

One other example of a social hook is *unique celebrations.* Why can't we have some of the best seasonal celebrations in town? The best, wildest, most fun, most creative Christmas party in town ought to be the one put on by your church or organization. During January or February, it is fun to have a winter beach party. Of course, the "beach" is in an appropriately decorated gym. We turn up the heat and ask everyone to come wearing their summer clothes. They wear their coats to the meeting, but when they take their coats off, they have their shorts and T-shirts on. Frisbees, volleyball, beach music, lifeguards, suntan lotion—they all help create the atmosphere of a winter beach party.

One meaningful activity our group did involved a mission rather than just a fun time. Through the local health office and Operation Head Start, we learned where there were families in our community whose income is under the poverty level. During December, we asked our teenagers to bring in all kinds of food and toys. We scheduled a Saturday for the kids to come and wrap the toys for the younger children. Then the kids delivered the packages to each family and caroled at each home. This "Care and Caroling" allowed young people to be involved in the entire Christmas project from collection to delivery—and it was attractive to unreached kids.

There are youth ministry resource books for sale that are loaded with great "packaging" ideas. This is not designed to be one of those books. The examples cited here are presented as illustrations of the *principles* of effective outreach programming. As we develop a plan to carry out our youth-targeted "Nehemiah Project," we must realize how important the social hook is to youth evangelism. It gives a *reason to come* to the young men and women it is our dream to reach.

A Place to Talk

The third item in the plan for reaching lost teenagers is *a place to talk*—like a weekend night coffeehouse. One church I know of opened a Friday night coffee house, which they call M.A.D. House . . . Make a Difference House. They have different Christian music groups come in, and they provide a place where kids can talk around the table in some small groups. The church has about fifty people, but 150 people come to M.A.D. House. This is a little church with a lot of vision. They are simply providing a place where kids searching for intimacy have a place to talk and connect to each other. Providing a talking place may also take the form of a hotline for kids to call or small group get-togethers in homes, led by volunteers and fed by pizza.

Getting Away

Another part of the rescue plan is *getting away*. No matter where young people live, they love to leave. This getaway instinct can be captured as a way to attract lost teenagers. Christians ought to be having the best trips. If you provide an attractive trip in an attractive place for an attractive price, non-Christian kids will be interested in getting away with your group.

Starting Younger

A fifth part of the plan is *starting younger*. What used to be the spiritual battles of college have become the battles of high school. What used to be the battles of high school are now the battles of the junior high years. I have always believed that there are four really good years to reach kids—the high school years. There are still four good years, but they are probably seventh, eighth, ninth, and tenth grades. By the time young people get a car, a license, a boyfriend or girlfriend, a job, a team, a sport, they start turning hard and less reachable.

Junior high young people need to be part of the rescue plan. They are teenagers in search of a social life. A church that provides an active junior high activity program, with the Gospel as a regular component of it, can attract a lot of kids. In contrast with high school ministry, it is important that a lot of parents be involved in the leadership. If you have parents involved in a high school group, it can hurt. But in junior high, young people are still parent dependent and they know that. So it is helpful to have a team of volunteer parents who each have an assignment—e.g., transportation, refreshments, program. This parent team provides the credibility other parents will be looking for before sending their son or daughter to your group.

If you are facing mostly blank stares and unresponsive attitudes from your high school group or you can't even find high-schoolers, it may be time to temporarily shift major energies to junior high age kids. It makes sense to start building or rebuilding a youth program with some young, pliable, impressionable junior high kids. Pretty soon they'll be high schoolers, and you can begin to affect the high school group through them. And when they start to become bored with youth group, they can graduate from being receivers to being older models and student leaders for the next junior high wave.

THE FIRE SPREADS: A MOBILIZED ARMY

As you begin to deploy the powerful weapons displayed in the Nehemiah Project, you will see the emergence of a dream and a plan. The dream—a vision for rescuing lost young people in your area. The plan—a strategy from God's heart to yours, consistent with your abilities and the kinds of kids to whom God is calling you. It starts to get exciting when a plan begins to emerge. But there is a dangerous tendency to rush past the first and second weapons and rush into a doing mode. We like methods, plans, formulas, and instant programs. But it all has to start with a broken heart. That is the fire that fuels everything else. Out of that heart will come a desperate prayer vigil that opens hearts, weakens strongholds—and births *God's* dream and *God's* plan.

The fourth weapon in the battle for a generation takes the fire for rescuing lost young people from one heart to many hearts. In the Nehemiah model, the leader reaches the point where he has gone as far as he can go alone. When Nehemiah got to Jerusalem, he went out on a little midnight tour of the city's devastated walls and gates. He took some of his Jewish brothers out with him. His unspoken goal—to help them feel the burden God has placed in his heart. As they surveyed the brokenness, Nehemiah said, "You see the trouble we are in: Jerusalem lies in ruins, and its gates have been burned with fire. Come, let us rebuild the wall of Jerusalem, and we will no longer be in disgrace" (Nehemiah 2:17). And the heart-fire spread. "They replied, 'Let us start rebuilding.' So they began this good work" (Nehemiah 2:18).

The following chapter in Nehemiah does not make the most exciting reading. It says things such as, "The Fish Gate was rebuilt by the sons of Hassenaah. They laid its beams," and "The next section was repaired by the men of Tekoa," and so on. This is not recommended reading when you are sleepy. But it makes a critical point. *Everyone* has owned the dream and the plan, from the princes to the peasants to the perfume makers. All the residents were rebuilding the corner near them.

We can see in this breakthrough the fourth weapon in winning the battle for young lives—*a mobilized army*. Though the burden often starts with one person, that broken heart needs to spread to the hearts of other believers. The job is too big for one man or woman to do alone.

In a sense, we have been taking a tour of our "devastated city"—the lives of today's teenagers. If that burden has gripped your heart, you need for it to grip others. Nehemiah encouraged that "heart transplant" by taking his future leadership on a tour of the need. Out of that tour was created a mobilized army where everyone was doing what he or she knew how to do in the interest of the cause. If someone lived near a gate, he could work on rebuilding that gate. If others lived near a certain part of the wall, they could work on rebuilding that part of the wall.

Your mission, if you choose to become a missionary to this generation, is to infect every person you can with heart trouble for lost young people. The result you pray for is that each one will do what he or she knows how to do to influence the young people in their corner.

Three Mobilized Groups

The mobilized army for youth outreach has three groups of people who need to own the mission. The first group is the *Christian teenagers*. The goal of most Christian young people today is not to spread their faith, but simply to survive spiritually. They are thinking, *If I can make it through I'll be OK. It's so bad out there and there is so much pressure. If I can just survive as a Christian until the end of high school, I will be doing well, right?* No!

Picture this Christian teenager staggering into the presence of Jesus one day with a bullet hole in his hat, his arm in a sling, and three tattered pages of the gospel of John in his hand. Jesus says, "Well, how'd you do?"

The young man whimpers, "I survived."

I can imagine Jesus' response: "You had the power of the Holy Spirit of God, a resurrected Christ, and the awesome God who created a hundred million galaxies in a moment, living inside of you. And all you could do was *survive?*"

Unfortunately, the unspoken goal of many churches for their youth ministry is just to help their believing kids survive. "If you can get them through high school and they don't get pregnant, don't use drugs, don't get drunk, and don't swear too much . . .

congratulations. You get a gold star and renewal of your contract for another year. Have lots of parties for them, fellowship, and take them roller skating. Do all kinds of stuff for them. Give them another social life so they don't get sucked into all those bad parties. Just get them through."

If the goal for our Christian young people is merely to survive, they probably won't. Survival is an unworthy goal for a person in whom there lives resurrection power! No, they don't need a survival kit. They need a *mission*.

Your Christian young people need to be taken on a tour of the needs of their friends, to see their friends as hopelessly lost without Jesus Christ. They need to be challenged to realize that Jesus goes to their school through them . . . that they as young believers are their friends' best hope for ever seeing heaven. This call to arms for Christian teenagers will be discussed more later, but it is important to realize that they must be the front line troops of any youth evangelism army. A mobilized army begins with them.

Second, the *leaders of your church* need to become part of the "wall builders." If the leadership of the church doesn't have heart trouble for the kids in your town, they may obstruct the rescue effort. Practically, they won't give you the money or the support; and they won't let you take the necessary risks or employ relevant methods. You will be on the defensive answering questions like— "How come you're not at the church? What are you doing over at the school? You're supposed to just be taking care of our kids. How come you're going over and meeting those other kids? We want you to make sure that the deacons' kids don't get pregnant. Why are you playing that music? How come you're doing all these games and crazy activities?"

The church leaders will have to be in this with you. How does that happen? Remember how Nehemiah got others started. He didn't start out with methods—"Here's a brick and a trowel." First, he showed them the *need*.

A few times each year I teach a seminar called "16 & Lost" at the Billy Graham Schools of Evangelism. The strong attendance and response shows a high level of interest on the part of pastors from all denominations. They really do care. But most of them are shocked when they hear where kids are today. They haven't been in a position to know. It's not their fault. But they are overwhelmed when they hear the desperation and paganness of today's young people. When I tell them the difference their churches could make, they are responsive. They say, "Yes, this is what we want." But I am convinced that many of them would not accept the strategy if they were not first presented with the need. If you do not start with the need, the church leaders will not understand the methods. Until they know what kids are like, they won't understand what you're doing to reach those kids.

In a sense, the burdened youth worker goes to the leadership of the church as a scout would report back to the wagon train. The leaders need to hear from someone who's been where they have not gone, who can explain what is out there.

As you carry the need you have seen back to the "wagon train," you can say, "I have to tell you what I've heard and seen—the lostness of the kids we drive by every day. . . that school we drive by all the time. Do you know what happens there? Do you know the desperation, the hurt, the pain, the lostness? We cannot leave them lost."

Once you've done that, there may well be leaders who will respond, "Yes! Let's rebuild the kids in our area. We've got to do something." But we, the scouts, must remember that the call to action is not methods. The call to action is a need that breaks your heart. It may help to show a video or to present a tape or a book or statistics. It might even be appropriate to let a couple of the church's Christian young people tell from their hearts about the lostness of their peers. Most important, pray that the God who broke your heart for lost kids will break their hearts too.

If your church could be challenged with the needs of teenagers and the urgent battle for a generation, it could send a current through the whole church. But it won't be your great plans or methods that will stir their hearts. It will be the moving realization of what it means to be sixteen and lost.

Where will the leaders of the church get a broken heart? On their knees, praying for the young mission field around them. Invite them to join you in a regular prayer time for the local high school and junior high school . . . for some specific lost kids . . . for the Christian teachers in that school . . . for what your Christian kids have to face when they go to that school.

The third part of that mobilized army, after the Christian kids and the leaders of your church, is *the rest of God's family in your town*. If we start to see the size of the wall that has to be rebuilt, we will realize that the job is going to require all the Christ-centered churches and ministries working together.

Unfortunately, turf and insecurity tend to keep God's people apart—even in a cause as urgent as the battle for a generation. We have a tendency to look at the kids in the church youth group and say, "These are *our* kids." That's wrong. They are *His* kids. When did they get to be ours? By being possessive of "our" kids, many churches are robbing their Christian young people of some much needed encouragement.

Joining Ranks

Take a second and draw a small circle diagram that represents the local high school. Here's Central High School. Let's assume that there are several Christ-centered churches in Central High School's area. For each church represented, put a small circle within the larger "school circle" with the number of kids involved. Perhaps First Church has thirty kids involved with a youth group. Second Church has twenty kids. Third Church is struggling with only ten kids. Fourth Church has a large youth group with eighty teenagers involved. At Central High School, there are one thousand kids.

Everyone's real worried about keeping "our" kids. In fact, the smaller the group, the more defensive they are about it, "We've only got ten. If we lose one, we'll only have nine." Everyone is saying, "What about our twenty? Or thirty?" The result of all this territorial narrowness is a tragedy in Great Commission math. All the groups together have a total of 140 young people in them . . . while there are 860 dying young people at Central High School whom *no one* is reaching! *They* must be the basis for youth ministries coming together.

The kids huddle together in their separate youth meetings and think, *So how many Christians are there in my school? I see four.*

They feel unnecessarily alone. But it would be so empowering if three groups of twenty could, for example, meet as a group of sixty once a month. The leader's fear of losing kids should not deprive his group from feeling the strength of "together power." Everyone would benefit.

Someone needs to begin a regular prayer gathering on behalf of lost young people—a fellowship that includes youth sponsors, youth leaders, pastors, youth pastors, Christian teachers, and any others touching young lives in your community. If you have the broken heart and the dream, that someone is you. Out of that prayer focus can come a "dream and a plan" that will be owned and implemented by a powerful mobilized army.

In the late 1980s, a helicopter with tourists aboard crashed into the East River in New York City. Two fire department scuba divers arrived first. They jumped into the river to rescue the people. About five minutes later nine scuba-geared police department divers arrived. They were on the dock, ready to go into the East River when the people from the fire department said, "We got it. We don't need you. We have it covered. This is our rescue."

The tragedy was that a man died in that helicopter at the bottom of the East River—while the people who could have saved his life were fighting over turf on the dock. Turf doesn't matter when *people are dying.* It is time for God's people to surrender turf, join efforts, and fight together for a generation of dying young people. The cost of not working together is too expensive.

WHATEVER IT TAKES

The victory of Nehemiah and his mobilized team underscores the last weapon for waging this battle for a generation—*an unwavering effort.* Nehemiah 4:6 records the leader's summary of their success—"So we rebuilt the wall till all of it reached half its height, for the people worked with all their heart." With all their heart—no matter what the enemy tried to do, no matter how many hours they had to work, no matter the setbacks. The Nehemiah Project succeeded because of a wholehearted, persevering effort.

So will the Battle for a Generation Project. If you want quick results or hazard-free driving, you will not stay with the battle long enough to win. This effort means patiently leading Christian teenagers who have a sense of mission and showing non-Christian teenagers they can trust you. Building relationships with kids, school administrators, teachers, coaches, and parents takes a consistent, hang-in-there effort. There will be highs and lows, victories and defeats, encouragements and discouragements each step of the way. But an unwavering "Nehemiah" effort can ultimately affect a community and capture many young lives for Jesus Christ.

A great biblical example for youth evangelism is found in the story of those four men who were determined to bring their paralyzed friend to Jesus (Mark 2:1–12). People were blocking the door and all the windows. There was no conventional means of getting this man to Jesus.

Did they say, "It's too tough. We were motivated, but we

couldn't get it done"? Not these wonderfully stubborn men! They started tearing up the roof and lowering their friend down into Jesus' presence. These innovative, determined men modeled what the rescuing of lost young people requires. Their motto was *"whatever it takes."*

That is the heartbeat of a warrior in the battle for a generation—"I will do whatever it takes to bring dying young people to Jesus. If I can't get them to Him in a conventional way, I will find a way that works. Failure is not an option."

Many influences will pull you back toward comfort, safety, and just taking care of the little flock. Most folks at church will be happy if you do that. There won't be anybody pushing you—except the broken heart of Jesus inside you. Without the broken heart, you'll start down this road, have a little success, a little failure, and probably drift back to what is easy. But I know from my own life that a broken heart can drive you for at least thirty-four years. You won't quit. You will do whatever it takes.

Winning this battle for the teenagers Jesus died for requires the most powerful of weapons. This is not "twenty-nine hot new methods for youth ministry." This battle requires the explosive combination that won in Nehemiah's day—a broken heart . . . a desperate prayer vigil . . . a dream and a plan . . . a mobilized army . . . and an unwavering effort. It's a big job. There are only a few people to do it. And there's a short time to get it done. But these weapons will win.

5

SERIOUS BUSINESS
... SERIOUS LEADERS

The grocery store today features "lite" everything—"lite" butter . . . "lite" bread . . . "lite" cheesecake. Unfortunately, a lot of skinny goodies are *flavor* lite too.

Somewhere along the way work with young people has gotten the image of being lightweight ministry—baby-sitting church kids, eating pizza, playing basketball, telling jokes, running activities, dispensing spiritual "snacks." But this battle for lives in their most decisive years is not a ministry picnic—it is *war*. It is not "practice" ministry where a person makes his or her rookie mistakes so he or she can be promoted to "real" ministry—with adults. This is the *front lines*. Rescuing and shaping young lives requires *warriors*.

An immature or irresponsible leader cannot hurt mature adults too much—but he or she can do lifelong damage to a teenager. Young people are easily hurt, easily used, easily misled, easily disillusioned.

Any person put in leadership over them will automatically become a role model—for better or worse. Because teenagers will observe their leader up close, that leader will define in flesh and blood for them what "follower of Christ" means—and they will copy what they see. The leader's strengths will give a teenager a mark to reach for. The leader's weaknesses will give a teenager tacit permission to be weak there too. Jesus made clear how He feels about an adult who misleads a young life—"If anyone causes one of these little ones who believe in me to sin, it would be better for him to have a large millstone hung around his neck and to be drowned in the depths of the sea" (Matthew 18:6).

Youth ministry is serious business. It demands serious leaders. The qualifications for youth leaders have far more to do with their *character* than their *charisma* . . . with their *godliness* than their *gifts*. Ultimately, it is not an activity director, "cool" guy, or overgrown teenager that our pliable young people desperately need. They need someone who can say with integrity, "Follow my example, as I follow the example of Christ" (1 Corinthians 11:1). It is significant that of fifteen characteristics listed as God's requirements for spiritual leaders, only *one* has anything to do with abilities ("able to teach")—the rest are all about *character* (1 Timothy 3:1-7).

Over the past thirty-plus years of ministry, I have seen virtually every flavor of youth leader. I have watched some shepherd teenagers into a transforming daily relationship with Jesus Christ . . . some who impressed them but left them unchanged . . . others who were just overgrown teenagers who reinforced the kids' immaturity . . . and still others who did irreparable damage by the selfish and sinful things they did in Jesus' name.

SEVEN COMMANDMENTS FOR YOUTH LEADERS

Out of these years of watching the "youth leader parade" going by, I have concluded there are some *non-negotiables* in the character of one who would shape young lives. They are so non-negotiable that I present them as *commandments*. Certainly, they do not carry a fraction of the authority intrinsic in those Ten Commandments that came down from Mt. Sinai. In fact, our list only makes it to seven. But they do summarize volumes of biblical teaching on God's requirements for His leaders. They should define any man or woman who shepherds His young sheep.

1. Do It for the Right Motives

Too many teenagers have been used or hurt by adults who worked with them for the wrong reasons. Some of the inadequate, but all too common, motives for being in youth ministry include:

(1) A hungry ego—needing the approval and admiration of teenagers to prop up one's own insecurities or unresolved "baggage." If you're in it to have *your* needs met, you are on the wrong mission. Youth ministry is all about *their* needs.

(2) An extended adolescence—the desire to be in a branch of the Lord's work where a person can continue the "fun and games"

and irresponsibility of adolescence. The last thing a teenager needs is an adult trying to *still be* a teenager.

(3) A frustrated Romeo or Juliet—a leader with a need to impress the opposite sex. Teenage girls or guys will fuel the ego of even the most socially unlikely youth leader because that leader gives them focused attention. But any man or woman in ministry who is seeking attention from the opposite sex is a moral accident looking for a place to happen.

Actually, any motive that is focused on the *leader's* needs is an unworthy, even dangerous, motive. And it is ultimately our *motive* that Jesus will judge, more than our work—"He will bring to light what is hidden in darkness and will expose the motives of men's hearts. At that time each will receive his praise from God" (1 Corinthians 4:5).

There are two motives that make a person someone Jesus can trust, parents can trust, and young people can trust. The first is a deep love for Jesus—"I'm here because I have to tell you about this One I love so much." The second is a deep love for young people—"I'm here because Jesus has put His love for you in my heart—I'm here because I care deeply about you." Or, in Bible words, "Christ's love compels [me]" (2 Corinthians 5:14).

2. Always Take the High Road

"Chariots of Fire" seemed an unlikely candidate for the Academy Award—but that quiet yet dramatic story of an athlete with non-negotiable convictions won the coveted "best picture" prize. Based on the true story of Scottish track and field star Eric Liddell, "Chariots" portrayed his rise to the threshold of Olympic glory—and his agonizing choice the day he learned he would have to run his event on Sunday, thus violating his deep belief about keeping the Lord's Day holy. Liddell stunned the 1924 Games with his refusal to go for the gold at the sacrifice of his Christian convictions. Decades later his courageous stand testified to another generation through a movie seen by millions.

Early in the movie, an older believer gives Eric Liddell a bit of advice that would later frame his Olympic stand. He said, "Compromise is the language of the devil." Years later, when the pressure was on—even from his future king—Eric Liddell boldly refused to speak that language.

It is a language unbecoming anyone who would run his spiritual race well—especially one who is being carefully watched by young people. When it comes to life issues, from handling money to relationships with the opposite sex to questionable methods, the biblical leader must always answer, "No compromise."

The second commandment for a youth leader is to *always take the high road.* Whenever there is an ethical or moral question, we must always err on the side of being careful, not careless. God describes the person He can trust as being "above reproach" (1 Timothy 3:2). God's leader realizes that the reputation of Jesus rides on him in the eyes of those who follow him. So there is no room for any "funny business" or cutting corners that could damage Jesus' name or cost God's full blessing on the ministry.

There is often an air of casualness about youth ministry—and it is OK for it to characterize the climate of the *program.* It is not OK if that casualness begins to infect moral and ethical choices. When it comes to how money is raised and handled, you always take the high road so there can be no accusation of wrongdoing. When it comes to activities and programs, you avoid any method that has a hint of the dirty, the gross, or the suggestive. In terms of the opposite sex, you never get in a situation alone with them, giving the enemy an opportunity to breed a devastating lie or rumor.

Our adversary is a prowling lion, and he is desperately looking for a way to discredit the name of Jesus and the ministry of someone who is making a difference. God's leader simply will not give the enemy any compromise with which to get into his ministry. He will avoid even the appearance of evil.

In "Chariots of Fire," Eric Liddell is given an opportunity to run another event—one for which he has not trained—on a later day. Just before he goes on to win the gold, another runner slips him a note at the starting block—"The Good Book says, 'He that honors Me, I will honor.'"

God did honor Eric Liddell for taking the high road. Those are the people for whom He reserves His highest blessing.

3. Always Avoid the Edge

In a sense, this third commandment is the flip side of choosing the high road. It is easy to be worn down and seduced by the easy, breezy morality of the youth culture. People tend to become like the culture in which they work. If that happens to an adult who is a missionary to modern youth culture, that leader will make some damaging mistakes.

Without even noticing, a youth leader can drift into humor that crosses the boundaries of good taste or godly purity. He or she can begin to justify seeing videos and movies that should never pollute a heart in which God's Spirit lives—all in the name of "seeing what the kids are watching."

The same logic can be used to try to justify listening regularly to the increasingly toxic music of the kids with whom we work. A shepherd cannot afford to be poisoned with the viruses that are slowly killing his sheep!

So many young lives have been deeply scarred by the moral fall of a youth leader. But seldom is such a fall sudden. It begins with "innocent" flirtations or "brotherly" hugs—steps toward the edge. And suddenly powerful urges, fantasies, and temptations are stirred up—sparks that await only the wind of opportunity to explode into a sexual fire. And many get burned.

Those who work as spiritual rescuers in the darkness of the youth culture cannot afford to allow any of that darkness *inside*. "Have nothing to do with the fruitless deeds of darkness," God's Word warns (Ephesians 5:11). And "be wise about what is good, and innocent about what is evil" (Romans 16:19). In other words, *avoid the edge*.

4. Prioritize the Family

This fourth commandment for youth leaders is rooted in God's demand that His leader be someone who can "manage his own family well. . . . If anyone does not know how to manage his own family, how can he take care of God's church?" (1 Timothy 3:4–5). A biblical leader realizes that his ministry begins at the "First Church of My House." The Lord is not interested in using someone who loses his mate or his children in the process of reaching someone else's children.

Gardens don't get overgrown because the owner plants weeds, but through neglect. Families get overgrown in the same way. Listening to the cries of teenagers, a leader can miss the whispers of his or her own family. Enjoying being a hero at youth group, a leader can avoid the hard work of a healthy marriage and family.

Trying to always "be there" for the kids you work with can make you "never there" for the kids who need you more than any others—your own. Neglecting the one to whom you promised the best of your love or the child who has no one else to call "Daddy" or "Mommy" is a sin, no matter how noble the ministry you are doing.

Tragically, today's young people are experts on family dysfunction, distance, and neglect. They desperately need to see a loving alternative in their leader's family. When your family is working, you give hope to the kids you lead. More than once I have had teenagers say something like this to me after a week of camp—"Do you know what really got to me this week?" I have waited expectantly to hear some gem from one of my talks. "It's the way you treated your wife," they have said to my surprise. Or, "the way you took time to be with your kids."

Family neglect is a subtle, quiet killer. You don't know the damage you've done until it's almost too late. So when someone steps up to youth ministry leadership, he or she must first make a conscious commitment to put the family first. That means putting your time with them in your datebook along with all your other important things . . . being there for the times that matter most to them . . . including them in ministry trips with you . . . giving them your best when you get home, not your leftovers . . . including them as well-informed prayer partners in your ministry. And it means being a spiritual leader for your family first. If you're not their shepherd, don't try to be anyone else's.

Whether or not a youth worker has a family of his or her own, God's leader must always support the family. The adult who sides with teenagers in their disrespect or rebellion against their parents is violating God's clear instruction to "honor your father and mother" (Ephesians 6:2). Joining teenagers in their negative attitude toward their families may win some points with them in the short run, but it will cost God's approval in the long run. It is always our responsibility as leaders to help reconnect young people to their families and build better communication. The youth leader cannot deal with a young person as an isolated individual. A youth worker must always seek to build bridges of communication back and forth with the parents or guardian of a young person, helping both sides learn how to communicate with each other.

There are instances, of course, when a leader may discover serious dysfuncion or even criminal behavior, such as physical or sexual abuse. In cases such as these, supporting the family may mean making a connection with people qualified to intervene—a counselor or a community agency, for example. Serious family "illness" cannot be left to cause more pain; it must be lovingly confronted and treated by someone who can begin the healing process.

In a broken world, the model of a loving, respectful family is one of the greatest gifts you can give the young people you lead—and one of your highest qualifications to lead them.

5. Never Sacrifice Truth for Love or Love for Truth

A salad dressed with vinegar would bite you before you could bite it. A salad that had only oil on it wouldn't be much of a treat either. But vinegar and oil together make a winning combination.

That's how it is with that life-changing recipe the Bible tells us to use—"speaking the truth in love" (Ephesians 4:15). Truth alone has a stinging bite. But love that comes without truth is just a coating of bland emotional oil. Teenagers desperately need the combination, but unfortunately, many leaders give them one without the other.

Some adults in youth ministry are quick with straight talk, candid confrontation, and Bible verses. Kids "know where they stand with me." They "know I don't beat around the bush." The truth comes through loud and clear—but often without a lot of love. When we confront young people—as we must do when they are out of bounds—they ought to feel *valued* by us, not *condemned*. "Man, I care about you too much to let you do something that's going to hurt you and that's going to hurt God. You're too valuable to do this." There is confrontation in Christ, but there is "no condemnation" in Christ (Romans 8:1).

Other youth leaders—probably the majority today—are great at making teenagers feel loved and supported . . . but too often at the expense of the truth. They fear losing young people by confronting them with the unpleasant truth. It is not pleasant to have someone tell you that you are unbuttoned or unzipped—but it's worse to not be told. When teenagers are emotionally or spiritually unbuttoned, we have to love them enough to tell them the truth.

Sometimes this tendency to "over-love" or "under-truth" is rooted in the leader's own fear of rejection. He or she *needs* that young person too much; the leader's own security and worth has become tied to acceptance by a teenager. And the price is the truth that could save a young person many scars later on.

In youth ministry, the "truth-ers" often aren't lovers, and the lovers aren't truthers. But God does not allow us to choose the one that is more comfortable for us—He *is* both, and He *demands* both. The adult who makes an eternal difference in young lives realizes the life-changing power of the dynamic ministry duo—truth that does not tear down and love that does not lower the standards.

6. Pray Things Done

Youth ministry people need to be the *prayingest people in the church.*

When it comes to fighting for young lives and defeating the darkness that holds them captive, the powerless p's will not work—programming, planning, promotion, and personalities.

But all too often, most of our youth ministry time and energy is poured into these "earth-methods" of getting things done. Ultimately, *prayer* is the only method with any real supernatural power to transform lives, hearts, families, and situations.

So the effective youth leader lives by this sixth commandment—*pray* things done. In the classic passage on spiritual warfare, God concludes the strategy for victory with these orders—"Pray in the Spirit on all occasions with all kinds of prayers and requests" (Ephesians 6:18). The mighty apostle Paul stresses in almost every letter "all my prayers for all of you" (Philippians 1:4). His most dynamic ministry may well have been his least visible one—his fervent intercession for those among whom he ministered.

Youth ministry people are, by nature, doers. Contemplative, meditative types are not usually attracted to the high energy world of teenagers. But doers tend to make the same mistake Martha, the patron saint of doers, made—not enough time at the feet of Jesus. And the Lord said that Mary's focused time with Him was "better" than Martha's frantic service for Him (Luke 10:42).

Those who lead young people will quickly burn out unless they learn to refuel in regular times of prayer. They will stumble under the burden of carrying all those kids' needs unless they consistently turn those kids over to the Lord in prayer. And though their ministry may be very active, it will be relatively powerless unless it begins in the throne room of God.

Through prayer, we access God's power to open hearts that would otherwise be closed . . . to open doors that otherwise would never open . . . to change hearts that have resisted every other force . . . to experience God's wisdom in making decisions that affect our lives and others.

It is no wonder that the persistent cry of Paul to his friends was, "Brothers, pray for us" (2 Thessalonians 3:1). That should be the repeated heart-cry of those in youth ministry to every believer they know. In fact, no one should enlist in the battle for a generation without a committed prayer team, covering him or her with the power and blood of Jesus.

7. Have a Love Affair with Jesus

Before Jesus commissioned Peter to "feed my lambs," He wanted to know only one thing—"Do you truly love me?" (John 21:15-17). That is still His defining question for those He would send to His "lambs." Not "Do you work hard?" or even "Do you love the kids?" He wants to know if your central passion is your personal love for Him. More than anything else in all the world, the kids you serve need you to be a Jesus-lover. When you minister among them, it needs to be simply you loving Jesus in front of them—the public overflow of your private times loving Him.

It is those thousand invisible mornings that make an ordinary person into a powerful leader for God. Mornings where you spend exclusive time with the Lord Jesus. Devotions? Bible reading time? Daily ritual? No. Time with the One you are growing to love a little more each day. You read His Word as if He were speaking the words to you from the other chair in your room. You journal your response back to Him, thinking through how you will specifically make Him Lord of this new day.

My time with Jesus took off when I bought a notebook and began my first daily Jesus-journal. After I had heard from Him through His Word and He had heard from me through prayer, I wrote to Him about what He had said to me. That was many years ago. We meet again each morning—and I record the results of our time together in my current Jesus-journal.

From that love relationship comes spiritual power. Even those first-century enemies of the faith "took note that these men [Peter and John] *had been with Jesus*" (Acts 4:13, italics added). And that's where their city-rocking, mountain-moving power came from.

The young people you shepherd will be able to tell if you have been with Jesus. There is a radiance, an authority, a sensitivity, a stability that is found only in those who have been with Him. If you are going to be His leader, then you must make your time with Him the *highest priority of your personal schedule.* Your Jesus-time will simply be a *non-negotiable.*

Then, when you speak with the teenagers that the Chief Shepherd has entrusted to you, you will feed them fresh truth that He has just passed through your soul. Because of your love affair with Jesus, you will have something to share that came from His heart, through your heart, to their heart.

ONLY ONE

In a sense, the character of an adult who can shepherd young people is summed up in one shining word—*integrity*. When I hear it, I think of one of the few concepts I remember from math class—an integer . . . one whole number.

When you are a leader with "integ-rity," there is *only one you*. You are the same person at home as you are in front of the youth group . . . the same person at work or at play as you are at church. When your spouse or child sees you in front of the kids at church, she does not sit there in amazement and ask, "Where did *this* guy come from? I wish we had him at home." Wherever you are, whomever you are with, it is always the same you—the one who is becoming more and more like Jesus.

And when your life has integrity, you are the same person *alone* that you are when others are watching. Let the cameras roll anytime, let the tape recorder capture any conversation—you have nothing to hide. There is only one you.

You have stepped up to the challenge of letting Christ build His character into you. And you bring to those young people in your care a life-transforming model—God with skin on—an authentic follower of Jesus within their reach. When you lead from character, you are the kind of person God says He will look to. His qualifications are all about who you *are*.

"This is the one I esteem: he who is humble and contrite in spirit, and trembles at my word" (Isaiah 66:2).

6

PRESENTING THE GOSPEL TO POST-CHRISTIAN TEENAGERS

It has been known to throw a calm seminar room into total chaos.

I call it "The Communication Game." I simply ask the folks in the room to get into pairs, each one with someone he or she does not know. On the overhead screen is a list of ten items to find out about each other, such as their mother's maiden name, what they like to do when it rains, their childhood nickname. I then explain they will have only thirty seconds to "interview" the other person and get their answers, followed by another thirty seconds when the other person can "interview" them. They are all set to go for it—until I add one last minute touch. They have to be at least ten feet apart the whole time. In a crowded room, this makes for many overlapping conversations. As soon as they are given a "go," we start playing obnoxiously loud music. Thus, the room is chaos. Partners are yelling back and forth to each other with fellow "yellers" all around them, all the time trying to get above the blaring music. It would be a good time to do a Bible study on the Tower of Babel.

As we debrief this exercise in communication frustration, we list the problems—too far apart . . . too many other voices . . . not enough time. Welcome to the world of communicating Jesus Christ to lost young people. They are so far away from the world of Christians . . . they are hearing so many other voices . . . there is not enough time. That in microcosm is the challenge of telling today's kids the life-or-death information of the Gospel.

That challenge drives us to find the ways that will express the Jesus-message most clearly, most concisely, and most completely. The challenge begins with our vocabulary. Many wonderful Bible words, like "sin," "Savior," "believe," and "born again," are either meaningless to today's teenagers or they have the wrong meaning. "Repent," "accept Christ," and "become a Christian" are also examples of Christian words that do not communicate to non-Christian teenagers. If we cannot explain the Gospel and words like these in nonreligious language, the young people we are trying to rescue may never get past our "Christianese."

Even our Christian kids are, at least in part, products of a pagan youth culture. We are missionaries to a post-Christian youth culture. We have the same challenge any missionary to a pagan culture has—how do we communicate the message of Jesus in the language of the "native"? It's OK to use those Christian words if you explain them. Sadly, in many cases with young people, it is not our message that's being rejected, it's our vocabulary. We have obscured this life-changing, life-saving Gospel in language only we understand.

As I speak to young people, I'm always asking myself, "How can I say this and illustrate it in a way that they will understand without discounting the full biblical meaning of it?" We want to modify the package without modifying the product. What we need is a way to present the Gospel that will plug right in to where kids are.

How can we effectively communicate the Gospel? How do we get across "Jesus Christ and Him crucified" in a way that will be understood by a post-Christian young person?

We need to begin with what matters most to teenagers today—*relationships*. It is effective to present the Gospel as a relationship. Every teenager understands, values, and longs for relationships. All young people know there's a relationship missing— someone who is supposed to be there, but isn't. They think it's a boyfriend, girlfriend, a best friend, a group of friends, a close family, someone to get married to, a baby. But no earth-person can fill the hole in their hearts. It's God that they are missing.

As messengers of Jesus' love, we have a Gospel that is all about life's most important relationship. When you talk about a love relationship, you are talking about something young people already care about. You are starting with a vacuum that they already sense.

Second Corinthians 5:19–20 sums up the Gospel in one

word—reconciliation. It says that we are messengers of a Gospel of reconciliation. *Reconciliation* is a relationship word. It is about a relationship that is broken and needs to be fixed. That is where the Gospel of Jesus Christ begins. This Gospel that is all about a relationship is not just an attempt to be culturally relevant—it is biblically accurate too.

Our life-saving message will point the way to ultimate relationship—in words a lost teenager can understand.

NO MORE HOLE IN YOUR HEART

The Relationship Gospel can best be presented in terms of four important discoveries about life's most important relationship. These are the ingredients that need to be included in a message to present to young people.

It's a Relationship You're Supposed to Have

Every young person knows that "someone's missing" feeling. Our Creator explains who is missing in Colossians 1:16—and tells us in six words why we are on this planet. "All things were [here are the six words] *created by Him and for Him*" (italics added). The verse is about Jesus Christ. So God says we were created by Jesus and for Jesus—and you are going to have a hole in your heart until you have Jesus. The missing Person is the One we were made by and made for. But why is He missing?

It's a Relationship You Don't Have

In God's words, "Your iniquities have separated you from your God" (Isaiah 59:2). Whatever this "sin" thing is, it has separated us from the One we need.

To understand sin, look at the middle letter, because the letter "i" is the essence of the problem of sin. Basically, I was created to function correctly only as I submit and allow God to run things. Instead I have said, "God, You run the universe. I will run me, thank You."

In other words, I was created to live for Him; I have chosen to live for me. I was put here to live God's way. Instead, I'm living my way, and that's what sin is. Sin is thousands of "I'll-be-God" decisions in everyday situations. Lying in spite of the fact God says to tell the truth. Disobeying parents when God's way is to honor them. Having sex before marriage instead of following God's directions to save it.

So that word "I" is our problem. We can picture the earth revolving around the sun. As long as the earth is revolving around the sun, we have warmth, color, seasons, and life. But what if the earth says, "Excuse me, but I'm tired of revolving around the sun"? The earth goes over to the side and says, "I have found a nice orbit of my own. Thank you." Eventually, all warmth, all color, all seasons, and all life will cease. Why? Because the earth was created to revolve around the sun. Being in its own orbit leads to death. That's exactly what the Bible says about us. We were created to revolve around God. We have instead gone off on our own orbit and revolved around ourselves. And "the wages of sin is death" (Romans 6:23)—death as in being cut off from God, the One we were made by and made for.

Earlier we saw that our message should *start with their need*. That need may be loneliness or inability to cope with pressure. Or possibly depression, bad relationships, fear of the future. Whatever that need is, it is ultimately traceable to the fact they are missing the relationship they were meant to have to fill the loneliness, cope with the pressure, take away the fear of death, and handle life.

Now you can explain that the reason for the symptom is the cancer of sin. They are experiencing the missingness of God—"the wages of sin." If we die with that sin-wall still there, we will spend forever without God. That is what the Bible calls hell. But that is not what God wants. He created us to have this relationship with Him, now and forever. Yes, we are supposed to have this most important relationship. But we do not have it because of our sin, the running of lives God was supposed to run. Which leads to the good news.

It's a Relationship You Can Have

First Peter 3:18 says, "Christ died for sins once for all, the righteous for the unrighteous, to bring you to God." If I were discussing this with a lost teenager, I might define righteous, then ask, "Now, who's the righteous? Who's the one who's got nothing wrong with Him in this story? Jesus. OK. Who's the unrighteous? Yeah, you and me. OK. Him for me." The result of Jesus dying, Him for us, is to "bring us to God." We are separated from Him, but something about Christ dying brings us to God. And that is where we need to be—where we were created to be.

Often I have used a simple example to explain to a teenager what Jesus did on the cross. You are in debt. Let's say you (we'll use the name Julie) owe $10,000 to the bank, and the banker calls you in and says, "Julie, it's your day to pay your bill."

You say, "OK, I have two quarters here. How can I pay?"

The banker says, "Nice try. I said $10,000, and you pay today."

Suddenly a stranger arrives on the scene and says, "Mr. Banker, I don't owe this bank anything. If you'll check, I don't have any bill here. I would like to pay Julie's bill for her."

The banker says, "Well, wait a minute. It's her debt and you want to pay it with your money?"

"Yes," says the stranger.

The banker says, "Well, Julie, that would be up to you. You decide. It's your bill. Do you want to pay it yourself, or would you like this man to pay it?"

You say, "Well, sir, I don't understand why you're doing this, but thank you very much." You allow the man the privilege of paying the bill.

You will not get a call from the banker tomorrow saying, "What about the $10,000, Julie?" You have a fresh start with the bank. Even though it was your bill, someone paid it.

I love to tell a young person, "That's exactly what happened when Jesus was dying on the cross. That was not just religious martyrdom. That was not some bad thing the Romans did to Him. This was His deliberate plan. It was His expression of love to say, 'You have a $10,000 bill with God. From all those times you've said, "I'll be God" or "My way." That's why I'm here.' All of those times added up. We end up with this tremendous gap between us and God. We have a bill that is unpayable. We come up and say, 'God, I'm a good Catholic. I'm a good Baptist. Did you know I went to catechism? Did you know I've been baptized? Did you know I've been confirmed?' God simply says, 'That's all counterfeit money. What are you going to do about your payment due?'

"Then Jesus comes along and says, 'I don't owe this bank anything. I have no sins of My own that I have to die for.' And He says, 'I will pay your bill. You accumulated the debt. I will pay it with My life.' At that point God turns to you and says, 'Well, what do you want? Do you want to take His payment, or do you want to try to make your own?' "

Of course, people are constantly trying to get to God by doing good things—that is why they need to see three of the most radical words in the Bible—"Not by works" (Ephesians 2:9). Most of the places of worship around the world would be empty next week if people understood those words. They're there because they want to earn salvation. But the One we have to reach says it is not by works. Not by Catholic works or Protestant works or Jewish works. Not by New Age works or Hindu or Muslim works. Not by anybody's works.

Most people's concept of dealing with God is like a man who does 80 mph in a 30 mph zone. He is pulled over and a policeman takes him into the judge. The judge says, "Are you guilty?"

The man answers, "Yes, but I don't have to pay."

And the judge says, "Oh? Would you like to explain that?"

The speeder's case is simple—"See, I've been through that speed zone a hundred other times and I've kept the speed limit every other time. So I don't have to pay for breaking it. Right?"

The judge says, "I don't care how many times you've kept it. What are you going to do about the time you broke it?"

No judge is going to accept good as payment for bad—including *the* Judge. The penalty still must be paid. No matter how much good you have done, you still have to deal with the times you broke God's laws. All the good in the world doesn't change that. You still have sin on your record. A young person needs to know that we are all facing a death penalty for running our own lives— and a death penalty can only be paid by someone dying. Someone did. God's one and only Son. The amazing center of the Good News is this: I did the sinning; Jesus did the dying.

Because of Him, we can trade in a death penalty we deserve for eternal life we don't deserve.

This story of life's most important relationship is simple but life-changing. It is a relationship you're supposed to have . . . you don't have because of running your own life . . . but you can have because of what Jesus did. The last discovery about this relationship decides whether or not the relationship becomes yours.

It's a Relationship You Must Choose

We can't have a one-way love affair. Love requires a response. So does the relationship offered by Jesus Christ. Sin was our choice, and having our sin taken away is also our choice.

How do we choose what Jesus did? John 3:16 explains the transaction of trading in death for life. This life-giving relationship belongs to anyone who "believes in Him." Since "believe" is not a word most post-Christian people understand properly, it needs a little illustrating.

Once when I was at the New Jersey shore for a conference, we suddenly saw the lifeguards running along the beach shouting, "Clear the beach. Everyone out of the water." It turned out that three children had gone out too close to the jetty and the current around the jetty had sucked them along. They were being pulled out to sea and were drowning. Lifeguards cleared out the water, and lifeguards were coming from everywhere along the beach. Some of them plunged into the surf in a boat. Other lifeguards ran out and swam as fast as they could.

When they got there, those kids knew what to do. They didn't say, "Thank you for coming," or "I believe you can help me." They grabbed the lifeguards, pinning all their hopes on them. Each one knew, "If he doesn't save me, I'm dead. I'm dying and this guy is my only hope." That's what God means when He says "believe." That is grabbing Jesus like a drowning person would grab a life-guard and saying, "Jesus, You are my only hope of ever getting rid of this sin problem, ever getting a relationship with God, ever getting to heaven. You are my only hope."

I tell teenagers there are five things they can do with Jesus. One choice is to reject Him and have nothing to do with Him. The number two choice is that they can ignore Him and say, "I'm busy right now, Jesus. I've got my parties, friends, sports, and all, so maybe later. But, right now I'm not interested." He's over there and they sort of know He's there, but they keep ignoring Him. A lot of people do that.

The third thing they can do with Jesus is to postpone Him. That's what many kids do. A lot of kids say, "One of these days I think I'll get around to God. That would be a good idea. I picture I'll be about seventy-five. I'll be on life support in a hospital some-where in intensive care and maybe I'll get around to it then."

The fourth thing they can do with Jesus is agree with Him. "Jesus, I believe all this stuff. I believe You are the Savior, and that You died for my sin. I believe You rose from the dead and that I need You as my Savior."

The last thing they can do is commit themselves to Him or pin all their hopes on Him.

The first four responses all end up the same place—away from God forever. Among church kids, the most common response to Jesus is to agree with Him. If you wonder why some of your kids are supposed to be alive and seem so dead, it may be because they simply agree with everything Jesus says. They agree with the sin thing, the Savior part, and that a person needs to accept Christ as personal Savior. They have no disagreement with Him. But you don't get saved by a lifeguard by just agreeing with him, "I believe you came to save me." Wonderful. Did you grab him? If you haven't grabbed him—trusted him completely to rescue you— you're still dying.

There are all kinds of church kids who have agreed with everything Jesus teaches, yet they have never grabbed Him as their Savior. They have never been to the Cross and said, "for me."

Jesus meets us one on one. It's a teenager at the Cross looking at Jesus and saying, "This is for me, isn't it? I take You for me, turning from what's kept me from You and turning to the only one who can bring me to God." As a person turns *to* Christ, he or she is also turning *from* whatever is in the other direction. If I want to face the sunset, I have to turn my back on the view to the east. A person cannot face two opposite directions at the same time. That is where the issue of repentance enters into "believing in Him." Acts 3:19 describes this process in these words: "Repent, then, and turn to God, so that your sins may be wiped out."

As a young person turns *to* God in saving faith, that person needs to realize he or she is turning *from* the sin and self-rule that killed God's Son. Instant perfection? No. But realizing that sin keeps us from the Relationship and that Jesus had to give His life to pay for that sin, a person changes his mind about living sinfully. Repentance recognizes that total trust in Jesus is not just an isolated spiritual experience but the beginning of a changed life.

It is our privilege, our eternal responsibility, to help each young person we work with make sure he or she has consciously placed all of his or her trust in Jesus for sin-rescue and a God-relationship. It is all too easy to be surrounded by Christianity and miss Christ.

I know a young woman who was a pastor's daughter. She would tell you that at the age of five, she accepted Christ— although there was no evidence of it in the way she lived. After a while she said, "Hey, I tried it; it doesn't work."

One day I had a meeting with her near her house. I said, "Cindy, would you tell me about this time you accepted Jesus when you were five?"

She said, "Yeah. Sure. Our Sunday school teacher had us all come up on the front row, and she said 'If you want to accept Jesus, here's a prayer.' Then she prayed that prayer out loud with us."

I said, "OK, and what exactly did you do then, Cindy?"

She said, "Um. I don't know."

I said, "Cindy, it sounds to me like your Sunday school teacher accepted Christ that day. You told me about a prayer *she* prayed. I don't hear anything you did with Jesus."

Cindy agreed with it all. She agreed with the Sunday school teacher's prayer. But she never told Jesus, "I'm giving me to You." All those years everyone in the church said, "She's a backslidden Christian." She wasn't a backslidden Christian—she didn't even know Christ.

Youth groups are filled with Cindys who have been around all this "accept Christ stuff," but they have never grabbed Him and pinned all their hopes on Him. They've never been to the cross and said those two words from Galatians 2:20, *"for me"*—"who gave himself for me." We cannot assume our nice church kids have moved from agreement to commitment. They each deserve an individual opportunity to make sure they have had their own personal walk up the hill—Skull Hill where Jesus is dying on that cross for their sin.

This is life's most important relationship. You are supposed to have it. You don't have it because of sin. You can have it because of what Jesus did. But you must choose in order to have it.

DELIVERY

I am not sure how an obstetrician feels, because I've never been one, but I've watched one deliver someone very important to me. I would guess that the most difficult, most dangerous moment in the process is the actual delivery.

If you have ever been involved in the process of trying to introduce someone to Christ, you know the birthing can be the awkward part. After you've shared the Gospel, now what are you going to do? How do you get the baby born? This moment in an actual human delivery is called crowning. The baby is ready to come. Now what?

For years I wondered how to best handle actually delivering the spiritual baby. This moment of delivery, this moment where a kid goes from death to life, from lost to saved is critical. What happens there?

It helps to walk through the process, imagining an actual conversation with someone who is at this "delivery point." In this scenario, I'm talking with Joe. I would start by asking Joe three questions. The first question is, *"Joe, do you want this relationship with God?"* Secondly, *"Joe, what do you think it would take to begin this relationship with God?"* This question is to make sure he understands. If he comes back and says, "Well, I'd better start going back to church," then I know I should describe again what pinning all your hopes on Jesus means. If Joe seems to understand, then it is time to ask, *"Are you ready to begin your relationship with God right now?"*

When a young person is ready to open his or her life to Jesus as Savior, the conversation might go something like this: "Joe, you actually get into God's family and have your sins forgiven when you tell Jesus you're pinning all your hopes on Him, in your own words. If you're ready to do that, here's what I'd like to do. Let me talk to Him first." I try to avoid the word "pray," not because it isn't a good word, but because of the religious baggage it introduces for so many people—ritual, prayer book, a certain prayer language. Prayer brings up different thoughts that get in people's way when they are first coming to Jesus. After I have prayed, I will say, "Now I'd like to ask you to talk to Him and put into words what it is you are saying to Jesus today about your life, your sin, and your belief in Him. If you're going to pin all your hopes on Him, you need to tell Him that."

At this point it is best to avoid the question, "Would you rather pray quietly or pray out loud?" Of course, most people would choose to pray quietly. But there is something confirming that happens when we put what's in our heart into words—like telling someone we care about that we love him. It is important for young people to hear themselves making this lifetime commitment—just as a bride or groom makes marriage vows out loud. It also confirms to you that he understands what he is doing—and it's a unique thrill to hear a young person's prayer of repentance and trust. If Joe is ready to trust Christ, I would tell him, "Since this is life's most important relationship, it will mean a lot more if you put into words that you want to begin it. Secondly, a month from now when you say, 'Did I really do that or not?' you could say, 'Yeah, I heard me do it.'"

It is quite possible that this young person may never have heard anybody talk to God in a natural way out of his heart. So it helps for you to pray first so he or she understands what it is like to talk to God. But keep it simple, reviewing the Gospel in your prayer.

The prayer of that teenager may be theologically unsophisticated—perhaps not as carefully worded as the prayer you could give the young person to read from a witness booklet. But prayer from the heart is what matters, expressing total trust in Jesus as the Rescuer from their sin. "It is with your heart that you believe and are justified" (Romans 10:10). One of the great prayers of the Bible is Peter's drowning cry, "Lord, save me!" (Matthew 14:30). And Jesus honored the unsophisticated prayer of the dying thief, "Remember me when you come into your kingdom" (Luke 23:42). A prayer from a sinner's heart means more than a prayer from the counselor's heart or booklet.

When the young person closed his eyes, he was lost. When he opens his eyes, if he has sincerely pinned all his hopes on Jesus, he is found. You have the privilege of being with him at the most important moment of his entire life . . . the most important moment of his eternity. Once you have tasted that, you'll want to be there for as many of those moments as you can. There is no greater thrill on earth than that. I pray that God will give you an insatiable appetite to deliver the Good News of Jesus to a generation that is dying of bad news, and to be there for them in the moment when they are ready to choose Christ.

It is not your job to *persuade* young people to put their faith in Jesus Christ. It *is* your job to *present* the Jesus-story in a way they can understand. Teenage hearts are longing for the Relationship that will finally fill the hole in their hearts—but they are looking for love in all the wrong places. We have in our hearts and our hands the message that will lead them to the *right* place—the Cross of Jesus Christ.

7

THE BOTTOM LINE IS HARVEST

The first—and only—time I ever milked a cow was a few years ago on a farm in South Dakota. It was part of a special "Alive!" radio program we were taping in a farm setting. So I got to play Farmer Boy on national radio. The cow was thrilled. I am sure she could tell the truth about me—I grew up City Boy.

This puts me at a distinct disadvantage in understanding some of Jesus' examples. Many of them are agricultural in nature. I have often been able to get some remedial education from my wife—Farm Girl. I have also been around many farmers over the years. I always try to learn from them—unfortunately, not enough to help a certain cow in South Dakota.

One agricultural analogy Jesus used often is "harvest." I grew up in an apartment on the south side of Chicago. All we ever harvested were cockroaches. But I have been eager to learn about harvest because Jesus continually used that image to describe His work on earth. For example, "The harvest is plentiful but the workers are few" (Matthew 9:37) . . . "Ask the Lord of the harvest, therefore, to send out workers into his harvest field" (v. 38) . . . "Open your eyes and look at the fields! They are ripe for harvest" (John 4:35).

When I ask farmers what they think of first when they hear the word "harvest," they most often respond, "ready." Apparently, Jesus is telling us that all around us are people He has made ready for Him. That certainly describes lost young people today. Yes, they are more lost than they have ever been . . . but they are more ready for Jesus than they have ever been too. The factors that have made them lost have also made them ready. In thirty-three years of farming in the harvest field of young people, I have never seen them more open and responsive to Jesus—if He is presented in a package and a language they can understand.

Harvest not only speaks of readiness; it also emphasizes *results*. The purpose of a farmer is not just to sow seed. He does all his hard work with the *result* in mind—bringing in the harvest. If we are going to be involved in the evangelism of young people, then we can never be satisfied with merely sowing Gospel seed. We will always be thinking harvest—actually bringing teenagers to a *commitment* to Christ, not merely an understanding of Him. Harvesting is built into evangelism. Too many youth leaders present the Gospel without asking young people for the verdict that is implicit in Jesus' message. But if we are to minister with the heart of Jesus, we must ask Him for a "harvest heart"—one that is active, not passive, in trying to take young people from death to life.

Mark 4:26–29 has a beautiful description of what God does in the harvest and what *we* are supposed to do. "This is what the kingdom of God is like. A man scatters seed on the ground." Since we are the farmer in this analogy, it is our responsibility to scatter seed on the ground. What does that mean in evangelism? Scattering seed on the ground means we need to preach and give a person the Gospel information.

It continues, "whether he sleeps or gets up, the seed sprouts and grows, though he does not know how. All by itself the soil produces grain—first the stalk, then the head, then the full kernel in the head." I get a whimsical image in my mind here of a farmer getting up and standing over the corn all night saying, "Come on. Grow. Grow." Of course, there is nothing he can do to help this happen.

This part of the harvest process is God's area. And the Holy Spirit is doing what the "farmer" could never do—"He [the Comforter] will convict the world of guilt in regard to sin and righteousness" (John 16:8). At this point in time, God is dealing with hardness, hang-ups, questions—walls are falling and a hard heart is becoming soft. A person who hadn't been interested in Jesus now finds himself going to sleep at night thinking about God. No human can do that. God mysteriously, invisibly is getting a young man or woman ready to make a decision about Jesus Christ.

As soon as the grain is ripe, who puts the sickle to it? The farmer is back again. He was there at the beginning, and he is there at the end. When the grain is ripe, he puts the sickle to it because the harvest—what God has made ready—has come. As God's evangelism farmers, we are to be actively involved in bringing in the harvest of people coming to Jesus Christ.

HARVEST METHODS

How do we move all of this from the wheat field to youth ministry? In practical terms, our responsibility is to continue to *provide a climate in which a ready person could easily accept Christ.* There needs to always be a ready opportunity for someone to come to Christ. I don't know who's ready, but as a harvester, I need to be asking questions, providing opportunities, extending invitations, giving, confronting, seeing who is ready, and letting young people have chances to respond. We haven't given the whole Gospel until we tell people how to actually *respond.* When the Philippian jailer asked Paul and Silas, "What must I do to be saved?" they replied, "Believe in the Lord Jesus, and you will be saved" (Acts 16:30–31).

It is important to explain often the *process* of accepting Christ, not just the *need* for accepting Him. There are a couple of helpful analogies to explain this process. The wedding analogy is one I have used many times. It's an excellent one, because I know that there was a day I went into a church not married and came out married—a day where I consciously chose Karen for myself. There was a process that led up to that day of conscious choosing for Karen and me. I didn't say, "Hi. What's your name? Will you marry me?" No, we didn't have a wedding the day we first got acquainted. There was a process whereby we learned about each other through courtship and engagement. But we did not belong to each other until that singular day of conscious commitment.

You might wonder about my stability if you asked me, "Ron, are you married?" and I replied, "I don't know." You would probably respond, "Ron, if you're married, you know you're married. Are you married or not?"

Then I say, "Well, I think a lot of her and I agree with almost everything she believes."

"That's wonderful," you would say, "But are you *married?*"

"Well, you know I've been around her all these years. I'm sure somewhere along the way we must have gotten married."

Obviously, people who are married know they're married, because it's a day of conscious choosing. It is the same way with a life commitment to Jesus Christ. You may not remember the actual day you gave yourself to Jesus, but if you don't know there *was* one, you didn't. A person knows if he makes a conscious choice or a conscious commitment.

Commitment or trust analogies such as this are helpful in explaining the process of "receiving Christ" and "believing in His name" (see John 1:12). It is part of a leader's commitment to continue to create a climate for harvest. You never know who might not have been ready last week but is ready this week. There may be someone who has never heard the Gospel before.

We don't know who is ready. Ready people don't walk in with green, red, or yellow lights on their forehead that let us know whether it's go, stop, or caution. So it's important for us to continue creating an opportunity where people could come to Christ. We never know when they're ready. So what's our job? Faithfully scatter good seed with the complete Gospel in it, and then regularly provide an atmosphere in which ready people can be harvested.

HARVEST MIND-SET

God gets it ready and God makes it possible. But we need to go out and work with the intention of bringing back results. That should be our mind-set—to go work in the field as a harvester. Will everything be ready when the harvester goes out? No, he'll walk past some of the crop and say, "This isn't ready yet. I won't harvest this." But he goes out with the intention of bringing back results.

In John 4:35, while Jesus' disciples were all worried about what Jesus was going to eat for lunch, He told them His spiritual food was more important than physical nourishment. At this time, the Samaritan village was on its way to Jesus, and He told the disciples, "Look, open your eyes, there's a harvest here." Jesus was saying, "You still don't see like I see. I see harvest. These are ready people coming here." It was time to bring hearts to Him.

Another example of pursuing results is found in Luke 5:10 when Jesus called Peter and said in effect, "I will make you fishers of men if you follow Me." He said to Peter, "I want you to follow Me to catch men." Jesus didn't just tell Peter to fish. He said, "Why does a fisherman go out? You go out to catch. I want you to go out with the intention of bringing back results."

It is not our right or responsibility to push anyone, because it is the Holy Spirit's work to *draw* someone to Christ. But we do need to seek and provide opportunities to respond. It's doing what Jesus says in Mark 4:29, "As soon as the grain is ripe, [the farmer] puts the sickle to it."

On some occasions when I speak, it seems like the organizers have planned for everything but the harvest. They have the spotlight, music group, stage, sound system, posters, fliers, and radio announcements. They have everything. Then I'll say, "Now let me go to the counseling room and see what you have there." More often than not, the organizers forgot the harvest, and therefore have no counseling room, counselors, or witness booklets.

This is like a farmer doing sowing and working all year and then leaving town. We should act like we're going to have some results, and therefore have a ministry strategy for harvesting. We need to be prepared to extend an invitation so people can respond if this is "the day of salvation" (2 Corinthians 6:2) for them.

For years, invitations were frequently given in Christian meetings, but nowadays, in most places we could go for months or years and never hear an invitation. There are few or no opportunities to receive Christ. It is important to find a middle ground somewhere. Constant invitations can become meaningless or manipulative, but infrequent or nonexistent invitations are a deadly overreaction.

The Bible shows us that Jesus was always helping people choose. He didn't just present the message and say, "Let Me know if you're interested. Here's My number . . . 1–800–Capernaum." A good example is what Jesus said to the rich young ruler about following Him, when the man in essence said, "I agree with it all." We would have filled out a commitment card on the rich young ruler and counted him as a decision. But instead of signing him up, Jesus said, "Sell all you have." Jesus was bringing this man to a moment of choosing—to a harvest moment. In that case, the man walked away. But the point is that Jesus touched the man where the issue was for him, called for a verdict, and provided a harvest opportunity.

As we've seen, Jesus again modeled this call for commitment with the woman of Samaria (John 4). She said, "Sir, give me this water." Most people would probably have said, "OK, pray this prayer. 'Dear Lord, I believe in Jesus . . .'" No. What did Jesus say? He said, "Go, call your husband and come back." We're thinking, *Jesus, don't do that. She's ready to make a commitment.* But Jesus said, "Wait a minute. We've got to deal with this husband issue."

The woman said, "Ah, I don't really have a husband right now."

And Jesus said, "I know." Again, the fact is that Jesus was helping her choose by saying, "Bring your husband." That's a loaded sentence that leads to a true harvest moment.

Jesus asked the disciples, "Tell Me, who do men say that I am?"

They responded, "Oh, well we've been taking a little survey and 42 percent say that you are John the Baptist, and 21 percent say that you are Elijah . . ."—and they give their report.

Then Jesus brought the issue to its bottom line, "Who do *you* say I am?" (see Matthew 16:13–16, italics added). Jesus was constantly calling for a verdict. A conscious choice was built into His message.

If we are going to follow Jesus' example of harvest-oriented ministry, we need to know *how*. I might volunteer to help a farmer friend bring in his harvest—I might even sense the urgency of getting it in—but City Boy would not be much help without some hows. Creating a climate for spiritual commitment requires an understanding of harvest *preparations*, harvest *seasons*, and harvest *tools*.

HARVEST PREPARATIONS

When those crops are ready, Farmer Man must have the barn ready, the workers ready, and the equipment ready. If he is not prepared for harvest, he will miss it. As we commit ourselves to our Savior's harvest, we need to begin by making important preparations.

First, *every volunteer on a youth ministry team needs to know how to lead someone to Christ*. Everyone on that team should be trained to be a harvester. Harvest is a lot of work. Everyone who works on a farm has to show up for harvest. We can't harvest alone, so it is critical to make sure everyone is prepared.

One reason for this training is that we never know which teenager is going to connect to which staff person. One young person might not feel comfortable with one person, but might feel comfortable with another volunteer, so it's important to equip that second volunteer to harvest. There is nothing noble about trying to be the solo, super harvester.

Second, it's vital to *be prepared to follow up*. We need to act like we're going to have some results. One time when I was speaking out West, the organizers ended up having 2,500 kids in a big arena. Denominations had worked together and had prayed a lot. When the salvation invitation was given, 275 of those young people instantly moved out from the bleachers and flooded the floor.

There was no rededication invitation given; it was simply a straight salvation message.

One of the biggest reasons there was such a tremendous response to the Gospel was that these people planned like there would be a harvest. They had never had a response that big, but they had counselor training in advance and ordered a lot of Bibles and follow-up material. They had even planned for an overflow counseling room. God is the sovereign Lord of the harvest, and He doesn't have to do it on one night—so if an overflow counseling room goes unused, that's OK. But it is better to be overprepared for a harvest, because God will send His babies to where He sees there is a prepared delivery room.

One follow-up event those organizers did was a Great Start Party, which our ministry trains people to lead. One week after the event, local planners have a Great Start breakfast or pizza party at a local restaurant or a local church. Organizers pay for it, not the invited teenagers. That night in the counseling room, a counselor gives a teenager a flier and a ticket to a Great Start Party. In the following week, that new believer receives an "I'm going, are you?" call from a Christian teenager, as well as a call from the counselor making sure there is transportation.

A Great Start Party presents the secrets of a great relationship with God. Our ministry provides a video in which I present those secrets. It's a stop-action video so the local leader can stop and say, "Now get in a small group and discuss this" between main points.

It's OK to be prepared and ready and not have anybody to follow up, but it's not OK to have people to follow up and not be ready. A key part of preparing for harvest is being ready for follow up.

Third, it's mountain-moving to *focus prayer on specific lost kids.* We're preparing for a harvest when we pray and bind the strong man's hands (Mark 3:27). When we pray for specific lost kids, we need to also get our kids praying that way. Our Christian young people should be challenged to begin praying even a month or two in advance before an outreach event. They need to be encouraged to pray, "Dear Lord, I pray for Greg. I pray You'll make his schedule available that Friday night and that he won't have to work. I pray You'll start to make things happen in his life right now that will make him ready for You. Lord, I pray that You will get him ready. Soften his heart and somehow make him interested. I'm going to pray for him for a month before I ever invite him. Then Lord, I pray that that night he will listen to every word that's said. I pray there will be no distractions. Lord, keep him in the meeting and make him open and I pray he'll be ready to accept Christ that night."

God may or may not have the harvest that night. That targeted person may or may not respond. An individual votes "yes" or "no" on Jesus. We're doing the part we can do, but God is the One who makes the seed grow. Night or day, no matter how hard we work, there is harvest preparation we can't do—but we focus on the parts we *can* do. And having prayed fervently to the Lord of the harvest, we leave the results with Him.

Fourth, if there's an outreach event, it's important to *train event counselors.* Nowadays, when I travel and speak somewhere, our ministry has a video to train people in how to lead someone to Christ in simple, non-religious language. For a great harvest, it's vital to make sure counselors are well-trained about how to lead someone to Christ and what to do in the counseling room. As organizers, we can't merely think of all the spotlights, the publicity, the programming and logistics, and forget why we're doing it. It is most important to have trained people to lead kids to Christ at harvest events.

Another way to prepare for harvest is to *think through how we're going to ask kids to respond.* We can't get to the end of a message or the end of a meeting and say, "Oh, let's see, what am I going to do here? How am I going to ask them to respond?" It's important to think that through. Are we going to ask them to fill out a reaction card? Are we going to ask them to pray a prayer in the meeting and then come forward? Are we going to ask a friend to come with a friend? Are we going to ask them to stand where they are? Are we going to ask them to pray quietly and tell us later? We need to think through logistically and physically how we're going to ask kids to respond. That's part of the preparation of what we're doing.

It's good to keep in mind that it's not our job to persuade them to come to Christ. Our job is to provide a climate in which they could come to Christ, the encouragement to do it, and the information they need to do it.

In many ways, the harvest is determined by the preparations that precede it. God is watching to see if we are ready to "put in the sickle."

HARVEST SEASONS

Over the years, I have observed that there seem to be certain seasons of the year when teenagers are more spiritually ready than others. This isn't in the Bible. What is in the Bible is the parable of the seed and the sower. In that parable, there is one thing that determines what happens to the seed—the ground. Not the seed and not the farmer. It's the condition the ground is in. There seem to be certain times of the year when the ground is more ready—when young people are "softer" toward the Gospel. Those are important times to provide specific opportunities to make a commitment to Christ.

One such time of the year is *December,* because of *Christmas.* Every church in America ought to plan on December being a harvest month. During December, people are more Christ-conscious than any other month of the year, whether they want to be or not. In the mall people are singing Christ-filled Christmas carols. On TV there are Christmas specials. Even the most secular people are hearing about Christ. It is a Christ-conscious time of the year, a time when hearts are soft. It also needs to be a time when Christians are presenting harvest events, activities, and outreaches. A high-energy, attractively promoted "Cool Yule Party" can be one of the best places of the year to present Jesus and a specific opportunity to come to Him.

Late winter, such as February and March, can also be a good time to talk to young people because they're in the long haul of the rest of the school year. Generally, the things they were excited about in September, they are not excited about anymore. Often, a lot of depression sets in at this time of the year. It's a blah, bleak time of year, with less distraction. By late winter, many teenagers have found that their expectations from this year have let them down. It's a great season for a youth leader to address depression and disappointment.

The *end of the school year* is another time we can capture for Christ, because it's a time for evaluation. It's a time to say, "Let's take a look at what you thought was going to be great this year . . . what was, what wasn't, and what regrets you have this year."

Often I've talked to kids about "The View from Mt. Senior." One interesting thing about seniors with their terminal case of senioritis is that once they're finally at the top they don't care, because the things they thought would be important don't mean that much anymore. Seniors have found out what really is valuable and what isn't. They know that a lot of things they thought were a big deal when they were freshmen don't matter much after all. A sensitive youth leader can make the most of this season. He can say, "Let me tell you some secrets every senior finds out. For example, your high school empire vanishes in one night. When you walk across the graduation platform, everything it took you four years to build is gone in an instant. You begin to think that there must be something more.

"All those achievements you received will have someone else's name on them next year. Another team will win. Someone else is a hero next year. Life is a lot like that. What's really important?" It's easy at such times to talk to kids about "What shall it profit a man if he gains the whole world and loses his soul."

At the end of the school year kids are ripe for some evaluating, as long as we don't do it the day of graduation or when summer vacation is beginning. They don't realize it, but their school year has been evidence of their need for Christ. While helping them think a little analytically about their year, we can help them see that they need something other than what they have tried so far. At the end of the year could come the end of their search—at the feet of Jesus.

Another harvest season time often comes when everyone is thinking about *a community tragedy*. In one of our local high schools, a young man dropped dead of a heart attack in gym class. The Christian leader who was working with young people from that high school changed his plans for that evening's get-together. That night he got the teenagers talking about, "How does it make you feel about your own life?" Often when there has been a suicide, death, accident, or some other tragedy, everyone that age thinks about it. There is a brief moment when kids will be soft. We need to be there with the Gospel in those moments where the ground is ready for that short time.

Even *major news events* can create harvest times. I remember the day that the space shuttle Challenger blew up. Most young people don't care much about the news, but when something like that happens, they're tuned in. They knew about the Persian Gulf War, and that scared them. When those kinds of things happen, some of the visual images are so pervasive that even teenagers who don't care about the world can't get away from seeing them. Those moments provide an opportunity to think about what's important in life.

Some of the greatest witness opportunities in the world are

when a youth worker or a teenager is going through a personal crisis. If a youth worker is going through a tough time, teenagers can see how he or she handles it, and that adult can tell them the Secret of his or her peace.

The worst thing that ever happened to our oldest son in high school was also the best thing that ever happened to our son in high school. Today, he would tell you that football was too high on his list, that it overshadowed too many other things in life, and that it was almost a god. Since he was five, he had dreamed of being a football player and had built his body up to be one of the strongest, fastest guys on the team. During his sophomore year he blew out his knee and it took a year to recover. He tried to rebuild himself and worked hard at it. Finally, while he was getting ready to go back to practice, a sports doctor said, "You should never again play football." I sat in the office and watched the death of a dream, while he and I cried together.

The rest of the team couldn't understand how he could handle that injury. They said, "How are you handling this? How are you putting your life back together? Football is our life." All he could answer was "Jesus." The crisis in his life was the greatest platform for the Gospel he ever had in high school. Maybe it's at the time of crisis in a teenager's life when a youth worker can share with him or her the difference that Christ would make in that crisis, if only the young person weren't trying to figure it out alone. By being there when a young person's world is falling apart, a caring adult may find unusually soft ground for Gospel seed and a life-stabilizing commitment.

Wise farmers watch the seasons—especially harvest season. Ultimately, the timing of a person's rebirth is out of human hands and totally in the hands of the sovereign Lord of the harvest. But as His harvesters, we need to be alert to those times when the grain is ripe.

HARVEST TOOLS

In Jesus' harvest analogy, He said we should "put the sickle to it." There are youth evangelism "sickles" that can increase our effectiveness in harvesting young people and bringing them home to Jesus.

Before looking at the tools, it is important to recognize a harvest problem with young people. Young people may come to a place where they respect their youth leader, have an interest in Christ, and agree with what they have heard, but unless that youth worker pushes a little bit, human nature is to procrastinate and postpone, especially for a generation that doesn't want to make a commitment. A caring youth leader will give a teenager some encouragement to make a decision. That is where the *harvest tools* come in.

In meetings, it's effective to have some *"do something" messages or talks*—at the end they're asked to do something if they want to accept Christ. One proven way to lead them to a response is through a reaction card. At evangelistic parenting seminars our ministry offers, we give out a reaction card at the end. I always lead people in a prayer to receive Christ. The way they tell us they made a commitment to Christ is by putting it on the reaction card. It's simple and effective to have a reaction card, but it's not good to use it every week. A 3 x 5 card can simply say, "My reaction is . . ." Then teenagers can be encouraged to write down what they think about what was discussed that night. Using these cards, the leader is able to chart where his or her teenagers are spiritually.

Planned Harvest Events

Another way to encourage harvest is *"changed-life testimonies."* It clarifies the commitment process when you interview a young person who has come to Christ and that person describes exactly how he did it. It is natural, then, to say to the group, "You heard what Kim said. Has there ever been a moment like that for you where you committed yourself personally to Jesus?"

Another harvest tool is *planned confrontations*. If you are working regularly with a group of teenagers, you need to get together with your leadership.team and say, "Before this year is over, we're going to personally give each one of these kids a chance to respond to Christ. We're not going to depend on the meeting to do it." In a relational generation, many young people will never come to Christ if we're depending on it happening in a group setting.

It's tempting to try to automate this process. It would be less threatening to us as leaders if we could approach it by saying, "Maybe I could bring in a great speaker and delegate this harvesting thing to a professional harvester." That will work for some of the kids, but the speaker who comes in will never have what a local youth leader has. He doesn't have the credibility; he wasn't there when the kid's mother was sick; he wasn't at his soccer match; he wasn't there when her boyfriend broke up with her. But that youth leader was there and has been "God with skin on" for that young person. That "there for you" adult has a unique position in that teenager's life. He or she doesn't have to be a seasoned super harvester to provide a commitment opportunity.

The Right Harvesters

There need to be some times when a youth director says to his leadership team, "We need to decide who's closest to each one of the kids in our groups, and we're going to go to each one during the year." As December and the end of the year approaches, it is time to plan for personal get-togethers with each regular attender.

Maybe a certain youth staff person has taken a teenager home from practice. Maybe a volunteer has done a favor for another kid. In those unique periods of time, it's important for a youth worker to look for an opportunity to say to a young person, "You've been coming all year, and we've been talking about this radical commitment to Jesus Christ. You know where I'm coming from—you hear my viewpoint all the time. But I don't get to hear yours. Where are you with all of this?"

One way that teenager can tell where he or she is at, is for their youth worker to draw the diagram with the cross bridge over the sin chasm—and say, "Did you know everyone in the world is in one of three places? Some people are over here on this side of the gap saying 'I don't have the relationship.' On the other side is 'I have begun this relationship with God.' The third choice is, 'I want to have it,' and that person is crossing the bridge over the gap. Which one would you say is you?"

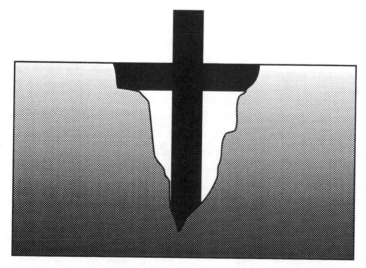

A leader with a harvest heart will help young people locate themselves in relation to Jesus, and not leave their response up to chance. To say, "Well, I presented the gospel all year and they never responded" is simply not good enough when the stakes are life-and-death. It's life-changing for a youth ministry team to go to each teenager individually and give him or her a one-on-one chance. That's a planned confrontation. Are we making them accept Christ? Are we pressuring them? No, but we are providing a climate in which that young person could accept Him. It's God's job to persuade them—we just need to give them a chance to respond.

The Right Time and Place

A change of scenery is another tool that can provide an opportunity for response. An out-of-town "getaway" can be an environment in which the voice of Jesus is heard louder and longer. Many times a change of scenery will help bring about a change of heart.

One other harvest tool to use occasionally is *a reminder of the dangers of not deciding*. It's not good to use this tool every week by telling stories of plane crashes or train wrecks or a teenager who suddenly died. But occasionally they need to be reminded of the dangers of waiting and not deciding to have this relationship. Jesus used the deaths of eighteen people in a tower collapse to tell people, "Unless you repent, you too will all perish" (Luke 13:5).

One danger of waiting is a hardened heart. Hebrews 4:7 is a verse teenagers need to hear. "Today, if you hear his voice, do not harden your hearts." Did that teenager hear His voice today? If so, he needs to be encouraged to not harden his heart. When someone says "no" to Jesus, he has made the next "no" easier and more likely. Someday his heart may be so hard it will be impenetrable. The Bible makes clear the peril of repeated rejection: "A man who remains stiff-necked after many rebukes will suddenly be destroyed—without remedy" (Proverbs 29:1).

There is a warning component in evangelism. The charge to one of God's Old Testament messengers has relevance for us today: "If the watchman sees the sword coming and does not blow the trumpet to warn the people . . . I will hold the watchman accountable . . ." (Ezekiel 33:6). While telling teenagers repeatedly about the love and forgiveness of Jesus Christ, we cannot keep neglecting the dangers of postponing or rejecting Jesus. There's the danger of a hardened heart, of not coming when Jesus is ready, and of dying without Christ. From the moment we go into eternity, our rejection of Christ is irreversible, as is our eternal separation from God. That is why God says, "Now is the time" (2 Corinthians 6:2).

The "sickles" of spiritual harvest among young people are encouragements and opportunities to exercise saving faith. Passive agreement with a leader's message or even with the Gospel will not change a teenager's eternal address. For each lost person, there must be a time of conscious commitment, of placing total trust in the rescue only Jesus can give. For each of us Gospel messengers, there must be a commitment to be active, not passive, in sowing Gospel seed and bringing in the harvest. The spirit of these harvest tools is that we go with the intention of bringing back results.

As workers in the youth harvest, we should never underestimate the power of praying for the teenagers around us. God can do in a minute what we couldn't do in ten years to open someone up and get him ready. We have no idea what we're getting done in a person's life when we are on our knees. We may feel like nothing's going on, but when we aim the power of the throne room of the universe at one teenager's need, something is going to move in that situation. While on our knees, we shouldn't be surprised if the Lord gives us an insight into how to break through to that teenager. Because of focused and fervent prayer, we may go to knock on the seemingly locked door of a young person's life and fall right in. "Pray for us, too, that God may open a door for our message" (Colossians 4:3). Prayer tears down walls, softens hearts, prepares the messenger, and prepares the listener. Harvest begins in the throne room of God. In the words of S. D. Gordon, "Prayer strikes the winning blow. Service is simply picking up the results."

Every harvest victory is pre-won on our knees.

A youth leader who understands harvest will pray and work with a deep sense of urgency.

A Minnesota farmer told me one October, "I wish I could come to your meetings. But it's harvest time. I only have ten days to make or break my year." There's nothing casual or laid back about a farmer who knows it's harvest time. The urgency should be even more compelling for one who is representing Jesus Christ to young people. Our time in their lives is so short. The season of their spiritual openness is so brief. And the price of our missing the harvest can be an eternity without Christ for a teenager we know.

When it's harvest time, you have nothing more important to do.

8

DISCIPLESHIP: CONNECTING THEIR BELIEFS TO THEIR BEHAVIOR

Some years ago, when my son Doug was about twelve, he and I were at a conference. While we were returning home from out West, he said, "Dad, I really, really liked this conference." My kids have to listen to me all the time, but Doug said, "Dad, I've heard you talk a lot, but it was different this time."

I asked, "How come?"

He said, "Well, you know what I learned this week? I learned that Christianity is like suntan lotion."

I thought, *Right. What in the world?* and asked, "How is it like suntan lotion?"

He continued, "Well, if you put a big old blob on your arm and leave it there, nothing will happen. It doesn't do any good until you rub it in."

He's right. Christianity doesn't do any good if it's a big blob of biblical truth on a heart, which it is for many young people and adults today. They have all the beliefs and right answers, but they've never rubbed it in. Until it's rubbed in, it doesn't change anything. It's disconnected belief.

When looking at many churched young people today, there are some serious causes for concern—evidence that the truth we are giving them is not changing their lives. It seems that most teenagers are not "rubbing it in." One proof of that is Josh McDowell's research cited earlier on the sexual behavior of conservative church kids. We know churched teenagers have not been taught sexual promiscuity in church. So, these statistics seem to indicate that though they've been taught one way, they haven't rubbed it in.

Many of us in youth ministry regularly face yawning apathy as we try to teach our young people God's truth. We have exciting news for them, but there's often only a blank stare and stony silence in return.

It's easy to see that many church kids are attracted by the lights of Sodom. It seems they're looking out the window saying, "If I ever had a chance and thought no one would catch me . . ." They know the things they hear and see are wrong, but the music, sights, and sounds have a tremendous magnetism.

The irony is that the road to Sodom is a two-way street. While Christian teenagers are thinking, *Hmm, that looks interesting over there,* people who have grown up and lived in Sodom are coming out saying, "Go back. It's an ambush! There's nothing there. Don't waste your time. I know all about Sodom and I can't get away from there fast enough since I've discovered Christ."

Another cause for alarm is the number of Christian young people who "lose their faith" as soon as they get away from the church environment and go to college. Could it be that many of them had no faith to lose? Possibly an environment to lose . . . or some "beliefs." But no real faith.

CONNECTING BEHAVIOR TO BELIEFS

What we face are kids who intellectually believe it all. They are not challenging the belief structure saying, "I don't believe Jesus Christ is the Son of God. I don't believe Christ rose from the dead or that the Bible is the Word of God." Most Christian young people would have a high rate of orthodoxy if they had a belief check. Many of them have never thought deeply about the implications of believing all of that, but they've signed up for the beliefs. However, their real life is their own department.

Sometimes I have wanted to say to a church kid—"Wait a minute. How could you believe that, but then listen to that kind of music?" A teenager thinks, *Because those are my beliefs, and this is my music.* It seems logical to ask—"How can you believe premarital sex is wrong and do it?" Once again, a kid thinks, *Because those are my beliefs. This is my boyfriend. This is my girlfriend. What's the problem?* Somehow they have managed to totally separate belief from behavior. They believe the beliefs and live like they want.

In the New Testament, the Epistles of Paul first address beliefs and then lifestyle. For example, in Ephesians, Paul takes three chapters and gives all the great beliefs about being chosen in

Christ before the foundation of the world, the unmeasurable love of God, and how the middle wall is down. Then he says, "Therefore, don't go to bed mad. Here's how you ought to treat your wife. Here's how you ought to treat your husband." Paul addresses what the beliefs are, but then he tells how we should live, *because* of what we believe. Believing is supposed to change our lives.

Today's teenagers say, "Here's my money. Here's how I treat my family. Here are my friends. And here is what I believe."

In trying to illustrate for young people how belief affects living, I have held up an apple pie, cut into six slices. Usually I have to fight off several guys backstage who want to consume my illustration before I can present it. With my pie in one hand, I spray a blob of whipped cream on one slice (of course, the kids want the can of whipped cream to "share" with their friends). When the teenagers are asked how many slices are going to have the taste of whipped cream, they wisely answer "one."

That is how many church young people want to approach Christ's role in their lives. They have an available slice—they would be happy to have that slice flavored by Jesus. But the things that really matter to them are represented by all the other slices—their money, friends, recreation, romantic life, music, how they treat their family, job, etc. With Jesus confined to His slice of the pie of their life, the other areas remain untouched by His influence. We ask, "Would you like to become a Christian?"

"Let me check," is the unspoken answer. "Oh yes, I have a slice I can spare. We'll write J-E-S-U-S on it. Now I have a Jesus slice!" Compartmentalized Christianity—the modern way to follow Jesus. We go and visit our Jesus-slice at church regularly—sing the songs, feel the feelings, review the beliefs. Then leave to live as we want in the other slices of life.

Of course, this is a distortion of the real thing. Jesus summed it up in this hard-hitting question—"Why do you call me 'Lord, Lord,' and do not *do* what I say?" (Luke 6:46, italics added). Jesus Christ is not Lord if we are not *doing* what He says. It's that simple. Back to my apple pie—before those vultures backstage get it. This time I hold up the pie and spray whipped cream on every slice. It is obvious to the teenagers in the room that the whipped cream influence has changed dramatically. Now *every* slice will be affected by the whipped cream. That is the picture of authentic Christianity, as revealed in God's Word. Romans 12:1 and 2, for example, calls us to "offer your bodies" . . . to "be transformed by the renewing of your mind" . . . and to "not conform any longer to the pattern of this world." Every area—physical, mental, social—is ruled and changed by the Master.

That is the kind of Jesus-relationship we must present to our Christian young people—one that changes the flavor of every slice. When Jesus touches every slice, He will change the way they treat their parents, how they treat their brothers and sisters, how they handle their money, what they do on a date, what they talk about, what they listen to and watch. That is lordship.

Jesus is called "Savior" 27 times in the New Testament and "Lord" 433 times. "Lord" is *kurios* in the Greek—"controller, boss, the one who decides where it will go, how it's going to be done." Unfortunately, in many lives today, there is no concept of Jesus being boss. There's only a concept of belief.

We have dealt extensively with how the church can counterattack the devil's schemes and rescue lost kids. But this is a war being fought on two fronts. The second front is the enemy's attempt to block Christian teenagers from living for Christ. That's all the devil needs to get a generation of his own. He doesn't need for everyone to be a non-Christian; he just needs Christian teenagers who aren't living it and non-Christian kids who don't know anything about it. From that point on, he can have all the following generations. We know from Scripture that ultimate victory is guaranteed, but we are losing individual battles in the war by our lack of preparation.

Probably the greatest obstacle in evangelizing teenagers is that many lost young people have never seen someone their age who's living as a Christian. Many times, lost kids cannot even picture what it would mean to accept Christ. They have no idea of what it means to look like a teenage Christian because they've never seen one.

Most kids are not about to become the first teenage Christian in their town. There may be a bunch of teenage Christians in that town, but if they haven't seen one, they don't know what one is like. If they do know a teenage Christian, they wonder, *Oh, you mean become like him. Like her?* But if they've never seen a Christian, they'll probably never see Christ.

What is our counterattack against the growing threat of spiritually neutralized Christian young people? It's called discipling. In this battle for a generation on the front that involves our Christian young people, we must counterattack with aggressive, purposeful discipling.

DISCIPLING—THE REAL LIFE CONNECTION

Discipling is the process of connecting a Christian's belief with his behavior. Discipling is not simply giving a person things to know; it is giving him or her things to do and to be.

Matthew 28:19, where we got our orders from the Lord, still stands, "Therefore go and make disciples of all nations." Notice where this heads, "baptizing them in the name of the Father and of the Son and of the Holy Spirit, and teaching them to obey everything I have commanded you." Here we find the key word in discipling: *Do* —"Teaching them to obey everything I have commanded you."

Discipling is not just the communication of information; it is about transformation. It's about someone doing what his or her teacher is doing. That teacher has not discipled someone if the person is not obeying. Joshua 1:8 (NKJV) says the way to have success is to "meditate in [God's law] day and night, that you may observe to do according to all that is written in it." Many times in modern Christianity, we observe to observe. We sit back thinking, *Hmm, interesting point.* We actually should be asking, *What do I need to* do *since I read this?*

We have to get beyond the little entertainment deal and three-ring circus we do each week for today's teenagers. They come to the meeting, sit back, and think like judges from the Olympics, *I think this week's meeting was a "4." Last week was a "4.5."* Sorry, but that's not discipling.

Discipling is a very honored Christian word that everyone is 100 percent for, but since many of us were never discipled, we have no idea what it is. We all believe in it, but what is it? That's what we will seek to define.

TWO INGREDIENTS FOR A LIFE-CHANGING MINISTRY

I believe there are two ingredients needed for a ministry that will be life-changing instead of just information-giving. Ultimately, these two things help teenagers integrate their beliefs and their behavior.

A Personal Mission

Without a personal mission, young people will sense no need to know what their youth leader is giving them.

Each year in late August, our local high school football team is outside practicing, sweating, and straining. At that point football is no fun. I have watched two sons go through this. When they came home from the first day of practice, they walked like Frankenstein, hurting in places they didn't even know they could hurt. They would say, "This is really tough." They would do triple sessions and pulse runs, then the coach told them things they were supposed to eat and not eat and what time they had to be in at night. He would kind of own their life for the next three months.

Imagine if at the end of the first day of practice, after they're sweaty and hurting all over, the coach says, "Guys, I want to announce one thing that's a little different this season. We're not going to have any games this year, but I will expect you to be at practice every day. We will be working out and I expect you to maintain the curfew and the diet." How many guys would be at practice the next day? Would anyone show up for the sweating and straining if there were no games?

The problem with most Christian young people is that they have no game. We keep giving them all the things they need to do as Christians—read the Bible, have devotions, study, pray, do God's will, do the right thing—but they have no reasons to do all that. There's no game to use it in. They need a mission.

Giving kids a mission will be discussed further, but for now it is important to recognize that a lot of the boredom and apathy is an appetite disorder. The reason many young believers don't have an appetite is that they're not getting any exercise. If a teenager is a spiritual couch potato, it's pretty hard to develop much of an appetite in him. By getting out, getting busy and working, a person works up an appetite and says, "Which way is the food?"

Today's Christian young people have been eating so much spiritual junk food that when we prepare a great meal—a lesson, Bible study, or youth meeting—they yawn and pick at it. They have no appetite and no exercise, and they've filled up on junk.

A Specific Faith

The second ingredient in getting teenagers to connect their beliefs to their behavior is that they need a specific faith. One of our great weaknesses in presenting the Christian life to people today is that it is so general. This is where the rhetoric gets into it. For example, we say, "Dedicate your life." Sounds good—but a little hard to attach to a typical teenage Monday. What is this thing called a "life" that I'm dedicating? And what is dedicate anyway? How would someone know if they gave Christ a life or not?

Teenagers need a concept of specific lordship instead of general lordship; specific dedication instead of general dedication; daily dedication instead of an annual dedication at camp, a conference, or a concert. That's why there are so many rededications. Some kids have dedicated their lives so much that they are up to their re-re-re-re-re-re-rededication of their life. A rededication for them has become a little fix that they get once or twice a year at some spiritual event that makes them feel better about the last six months when they haven't been living for Christ. Usually, in another six months they'll get a new rededication fix.

One of the guys I went to college with always got excited when a school break was coming, because he was about to see the woman he loved. He would say, "We're going to have a great time. I can't wait to be with her." He would get more passionate about going home as the days passed.

When he returned from break, we'd ask, "How'd it go?"

He'd say, "Oh, it was OK. It was good to see her."

We would ask, "What do you mean? We expected a little more enthusiasm from you."

He'd say, "You know what happened? Because we'd been apart, it took us the whole week to get back to where we were when I first left. It took all that time to get back to zero."

That's what happens spiritually to teenagers when they're depending on the binges and the spiritual highs to keep them going. They've substituted spiritual highs for spiritual reality. Consequently they keep getting back to zero spiritually. They don't ever make any progress with Christ. They have a quick fix: "I liked the music. The speaker was real challenging. I went forward and gave my life. I'm not sure what that means exactly, but I really do mean it."

Are they insincere? No, they are sincere, but they don't know how to put it to work. They need to be given a concept of lordship that focuses on one specific piece of their life each day.

In a youth outreach group I directed years ago, a young woman took two years to come to Christ. But when she did, she came on strong. After a week or two of being a Christian, she asked me, "Ron, could you give me a way to convince my big sister Sue* that this is for real?"

Sue would say to her, "Oh, Ann, you'll get over this. Last week it was a drug. Next week it'll be a boy. This week it's Jesus. You'll get over that."

---

* all names changed

So Ann asked me, "Could you give me an argument?"

I said, "I could, but I won't, because I don't think that's what you need. I want you to ask yourself this question, 'What change could I ask Jesus to make in me specifically that Sue would notice?'"

She said, "I've got it."

She left, and two weeks later I asked, "How'd it go with Sue?"

She said, "Great; I gave God the chair."

I said, "You what?"

She said, "I gave God the chair. See, we've got this big, red overstuffed chair in our living room. It's right in front of the TV set and right by the picture window. Whenever Sue and I start fighting, it seems that arguing over who's going to get the chair always starts it. We argue back and forth over the chair, and then we start arguing about everything. So, I decided that if I asked God to make me unselfish about the chair that Sue would notice. Now Sue is saying, 'Ann, what's happened to you?' She noticed! That was better than an argument."

Two years later, this gal came back to me with Sue, her older sister, and Sue said, "Ron, Ann and I wanted to give you the good news. I've made Christ my own Savior."

What Ann realized in her first two weeks as a Christian, many people don't learn in twenty years. She learned that Christ is the Lord of real stuff like chairs. Only Christ can give an unselfishness about something in a person's family and daily living. We don't just give Christ our whole lives, whatever that may be, because there needs to be specific lordship. Our job is to help a young person consciously make Christ Lord of the way he treats his sister for one twenty-four hour period of time. It might be a relationship, a particular bad habit, or anything he can practically make Jesus Lord of in his life for that day in that specific area.

MEASURABLE DISCIPLESHIP

On one hand, they do need to say, "He is Lord of my life." He can have anything He wants, but that has to be converted into something. Every time they come across that specific thing in their day, His lordship becomes a real flesh-and-blood-you-can-touch-it-you-can-taste-it-you-can-handle-it-you-can-measure-it type of issue, like the chair. Specific lordship is what will help teenagers get discipled.

After many days of lordship in a specific area of one's life, long-term transformations will occur. The effect of successive days with Jesus conquering the tough spots in our lives ultimately leads to a powerful lifetime walk with Christ. The continually growing lordship of Christ means He's Lord of a little more today than yesterday. That is, I don't surrender my relationship with my sister today, knowing that tomorrow I can "make up for it" by being rude to her again and moving onto another area to work on for one day. I submit my relationship with her to Christ's lordship, one day at a time, until it becomes second nature and I can concentrate on another area. Cumulative yielding is the impact of turning specific parts of my life over to Him every day.

As long as we keep dedication and consecration general, we can hide in generality from the demands of Christ. A person doesn't ever have to deal with the demands of Christ as long as he can keep them general. It's when Christ starts to connect with all those life compartments that living the Christian life becomes something real.

How does a teenager know what to give Him? He has to read God's Book. James 1 says that the Bible is a mirror, and we look in a mirror to see what needs work (vv. 23–25). This "what does Jesus want to work on today?" approach to Scripture gives a young person a purpose for devotions—which is often just another general Christian word without definition.

There's a reason for a teenager to sit down and say, "Lord, I want You to apply what I'm reading today to some specific area of my life. Then I will know that's the piece You want me to consciously make You Lord of today."

Wouldn't it be nice to have been one of the twelve disciples, waking up in the morning and saying, "Where are we going today, Jesus? Where would You like to go?" Well, we can ask that, but only through His Book. Encourage a teenager to ask Jesus, "Where do You want to go in my life today? What part do You want to touch today? Where can I touch You?"

In Joshua 5, when the angel of the Lord stood in front of Joshua on the eve of the battle of Jericho, Joshua asked, "What message does my Lord have for his servant?" (v. 14). That's how we need to read the Bible. That's a question to ask every time we open it. This kind of active growth brings "dedication" out of the clouds of generality and into this twenty-four hours.

Prayer is another area that is often presented to young people in general terms. They need to be taught about *specific* prayer. Our prayers are so general we wouldn't know an answer if it jumped up at us. "Lord, bless us." What is a "bless," and how would we know if it came? It's hard to spot a blessing when it goes by.

We pray, "Lord, bless the missionaries." Which missionaries and what was the bless? What exactly do we want to have happen? There is even a language for prayer that is only prayer language. We don't talk any other time like we talk when we pray. For example, we pray for "traveling mercies." When was the last time you said to someone, "Have some nice traveling mercies today"? Only when Christians pray do they talk like that.

Much of our prayer is so general and predictable that it is meaningless or not very daring. Teenagers need to be taught about specific prayer. Philippians 4:6–7 says, "Do not be anxious about anything," but pray about everything. And, "Present your requests to God." Anxieties are specific. If someone asked you what three things you were currently worried about, you wouldn't name general things like "my life." We worry about specific things, like paying a bill. According to that verse, God wants prayer as specific as our anxieties. It's important to teach young people to know what they're asking and bringing to God when they pray.

Hebrews 4:16 is the invitation to come boldly to the throne of grace. It says, "That we may receive mercy and find grace to help us in our time of need." It's awesome to bring God's great power down to one specific moment of need. "Be specific with Me," the Lord is saying. Teenagers need to learn the power of specific prayer.

HOW YOUNG PEOPLE GET DISCIPLED

The word "discipling" itself suffers from a great deal of undefined generality. Every youth leader knows he or she is *supposed* to be doing it, but many do not know if they are or how they would. The process of discipling a young person—connecting his or her beliefs to his or her behavior—needs to be broken down into practical steps we can understand and put to work.

The process of discipling is not something that can be done from a platform. It's not generally done in a meeting or through a program. It is done through personal contact, and it is an up-close transfer process.

My wife has done some photography, and she has explained to me about contact prints. When I take my film to be processed, I understand that basically the film is put directly against untouched photographic paper. Unless the film and paper are completely touching, there won't be any transfer.

That's exactly what discipling is. There will not be any transfer of Christlikeness from one person's life to another person's life unless there is direct contact. There is no way to do large-scale discipling. Paul discipled Timothy individually, letting him into his life.

Can a youth worker disciple a small group? Sure. Jesus did. In fact, the Master's model of discipling was generally done in a group of twelve or a group of three, though He did take individual time with them too. Either can be effective. Some advantages of group discipling are that it saves time; a teenager knows he or she is not alone; it can be less threatening; and there is built-in accountability. As Ecclesiastes 4:9–10 says, "Two are better than one. . . . If one falls down, his friend can help him up."

A strong advantage with a small group is that there's not only accountability to the adult leader, but there's also a kind of positive peer pressure. Often, peer pressure can get everyone feeling like the wrong thing is the thing to do. Well, couldn't peer pressure be used for good in a discipling way? A teenager begins to think, "Everyone's doing the right thing in this group, so that's a good reason for me to do it too."

Jesus is the Inventor of Christian discipling. As we watch Him bring His disciples from raw material to world-changing leaders, we can understand the discipling process in living color. It can be broken down into five specific steps.

Let Them Inside Your Life

Look at what Jesus did with the twelve disciples (eleven once Judas deserted). He provides the best model for up close discipling. Here are eleven average guys who ended up turning the world upside down in a generation by the effects of their work. All of us should be encouraged, because Jesus did not start with prefabricated heroes. He had very raw material, yet it worked well.

What did He do? He let them inside His life. He took the disciples with Him, and they saw Him angry when He was in the temple overthrowing tables. The disciples saw Jesus dealing with grief when He cried at the tomb of Lazarus. They saw Him struggle with distress as He went through the awful experience at Gethsemane. He didn't go alone to the garden; He took three guys with Him for support. They were able to see Jesus struggling with God's plan and Jesus' response to it. He let them see how He dealt with His family as His mother and brothers came and made demands on Him. They saw how He dealt with His stressful schedule when people were on every side tugging on Him saying, "Jesus, over here. No, wait, Jesus—over here; I need You."

Everywhere Jesus let the disciples inside His life. That's how they became what they became. They weren't merely a class that sat and discussed the ramifications of what He was teaching. He did teach, but it was always a totally integrated learning experience where they would know and do, know and do, often on the same day. Jesus modeled for us that discipling is the connecting of beliefs to behavior.

It's an invisible process that is not measurable, but it is powerful. It's the contact print transferring the image. The disciples might be called the "hang-around gang." They hung around Jesus all the time and watched the Word become flesh. There's no way a meeting could do that. That kind of life-availability allows potential disciples a front-row view of someone connecting beliefs to behavior.

Take Them Where You Go

The second step in the discipling process also comes from Jesus' model, which is *take them where you go*. It's important to make a conscious commitment that when you are going somewhere, you ask, "Who could I take with me? Is there something I'm doing right now that I could take one or two of the kids with me to do?"

What was the disciples' job description? Mark 3:14 gives it, when it says that "He appointed twelve—designating them apostles—that they might be with him." "Lord, what's our job?"

He says, "Be with Me."

"Yeah, but what would You like us to do?"

Jesus simply says, "Be with Me."

The first job of a disciple is *just to be with the person who's discipling him*. Mark 3:14 goes on to say that Christ sent them out to preach. They didn't go out to preach immediately; first they had to be with Him. Jesus said, "Come on, wherever I'm going, you go."

I have heard that if all of the elapsed time in the Gospels was added up, there is probably only about three or four months recorded. What did Jesus and the disciples do for the other two years and several months? I think they walked and talked. To write that they were walking and walking does not make for exciting Bible verses, but as we read the Bible, we see they traveled from place to place. We zip by that in the Bible, but they walked and talked everywhere.

There was an evident fellowship base to Jesus' ministry when He said, "Come and be together with Me." It's easy to picture Jesus and the disciples as they're walking, talking about the economy, getting money for groceries, what's going on in Rome, perhaps the latest joke, along with the spiritual conversations recorded in the Bible. There was a lot of everyday stuff going on, because Jesus took them where He went.

The process of discipling says, "I'm going to the store. Why don't I call her? I'm going to the mall. Why don't I take him with me? I'm going to go over and play miniature golf. Why don't I take . . . ?" It's a mind-set that says, "Whenever possible, I'm going to take someone along with me from the group that I'm discipling."

There doesn't necessarily have to be a heavy, spiritual agenda during those moments together, where we think, "While we're together, I want to give them three truths about predestination." That's a little tough over miniature golf. The point is that a discipler shouldn't go many places alone but should capture those moments.

This natural process of transferring spiritual truth is simply the classroom of everyday life. That is where the most truth gets communicated. God describes this in Deuteronomy 6:6–7, and even though the passage is addressed to parents, the principle is still true for disciplers in general. "These commandments that I give you today are to be upon your hearts. Impress them on your children. Talk about them when you sit at home and when you walk along the road, when you lie down and when you get up." See how natural it is? Doing things together provides the best atmosphere in which to communicate truth.

Challenge Their Faith

The third step in the process of discipling, following the Master's model, is to *challenge their faith*. Jesus does this over and over again. As we've seen, in Matthew 16 Jesus asks the disciples who everyone says He is, "Who do people say the Son of Man is?" As they start giving their report on the surveys, He asks, "Who do *you* say I am?" He is constantly challenging their faith, saying, "Wait a minute. How do *you* understand this?"

One reason there is often such reticence from Christian young people to express themselves is because they are hung up on two words: supposed to. "What am I supposed to say?" It's smart to think of that when talking to them. They're sitting there—as many adults also have done—processing what the leader is looking for.

They're not giving their answer, what they believe, or what they've come to grips with; instead, they're thinking, "What is the correct answer? How am I supposed to act? What am I supposed to say?"

Young people need to hear over and over again, "The only answer you're supposed to give is what you're really feeling. I don't want to hear any magic or learned answers from you. What do you think? I don't care if it's the opposite of what I think. Give me the truth." An effective youth worker will challenge teenagers' faith and get them beyond the words to understanding. Ephesians 5:17 says, "Understand what the Lord's will is." That should be our goal as adults who care about young people.

Several years ago a speaker at a youth camp said at the end of his session, "Guys, I want you to give me all of the unique reasons for being a Christian. In other words, no Buddhist, Muslim, or anyone else would talk about these. What would be unique reasons to be a Christian? Convince me." The answers started coming, which he wrote on a blackboard: "forgiveness of your sins," "eternal life," "peace," "happiness," and more.

When he was done he said, "Now let's erase all of these that are not unique to Christianity. There would be a concept of getting your sins forgiven if you did the right thing in other religions, so let's erase it. Eternal life, well they're all aiming for that." By the time he was done, the board was empty and there were no reasons left to be a Christian over anything else. He stepped to the edge of the platform, and said, "See you tomorrow morning."

Many youth leaders would say, "Hey, fire this man and send him home. He's supposed to give answers. Teenagers don't want questions; they want answers."

It was interesting around camp that day hearing, "Why should we be a Christian?" Guess what he was shooting for? Right answers or understanding? He was shooting for understanding. By the next morning, do you think they had an appetite? Yes, they did, and I was glad he had left them hanging.

That morning he began to talk about the two unique things in Christianity: the concept of *grace,* how God came for us instead of us going for Him; and the *resurrection.* The point is not just to do that exercise. The point is that he knew that what people need is understanding.

So don't accept rhetoric from teenagers. If they give a rhetoric answer, it's smart to make them define it. If they say, "Oh, consecration," say, "That's a word I've heard a lot. What does that mean? How would you consecrate your life?" Young people will think, *What? I gave the right answer. Leave me alone.*

What does a youth worker mean by saying, "You need to have devotions"? Sometimes a young person might give a pat, Christian answer, so a good response would be, "You realize that 90 percent of the teenagers in your school would not accept what you just said. Why should I?" That teenager will be thinking, *Hey, no fair.*

The first couple of times doing that, it's not good to put one kid on the spot. It's a wise move to do it for the whole group. If the focus is on one person, saying, "Paul, what did you mean by that?" the teenagers will begin to feel that they're being punished for giving an answer. Instead, it's better for a youth worker to ask the whole group, "How would we define that word? Most of your friends don't believe that. Why should I? Convince me, and make me believe this. Where does it say that in the Bible?" Maybe the group won't be able to tell where it is in the Bible, so a youth worker can say, "Well, I don't know why I should believe it if you can't tell me where it is in the Bible. Maybe after our time together I can direct you to some verses, but make sure you base your beliefs and choices on what's found in the Bible. Don't base your life on what you can't find in God's Word or what contradicts the Bible."

When challenging the faith of teenagers, success does not mean they offer the right answers. This generation, full of right answers, is living wrong lives. Answers don't do it. Understanding is what does it. "Why do you believe that? Why is that true?" When young people can define those words, give solid reasons for their beliefs, and support them biblically, they're finally understanding.

Why is this so important? Because someone in life will challenge their faith. It would be better if the first challenge to their faith should come from a friend of Jesus instead of from an enemy of Jesus. We can be sure that somewhere along the way, an enemy of Jesus is going to challenge their beliefs.

A class in a local high school was taught by a man who had studied for the priesthood and had ended up an atheist. His students would say, "Well, he must know. He studied seven years for the priesthood and he doesn't believe in God." One time he asked me to come in and present the Christian viewpoint, which surprised me, but we had a kind of mutual respect. One day he said to me, "Ron, something I've noticed about kids is that there are what you call born-again Christians, and then I've got ranges of kids in my class who are everything else, including atheists and agnostics." He said, "You know what they all have in common? None of them knows why they are what they are. They're just a category."

Someone says, "I'm an atheist." "Why?" "Oh, I just don't believe in God." "Why?" Another person claims, "I'm a Christian." "Why?" "My parents and church say I am." It's all secondhand stuff. No one knows why they are what they are, and they need to know why.

By challenging teenagers' faith, we're not shaking them up or destroying their faith. We're simply helping them think through their faith and make it their own. An unchallenged faith isn't *owned*. That's why our Master tested the faith of His own men.

Confront Their Soft Spots

The fourth step in the discipling process is to *confront their soft spots*. An example of that is in Luke 8:24–25. Numerous examples can be found in Jesus' work with His disciples, such as when they saw Jesus feed five thousand people. Well, here are the disciples out on the lake and a storm comes up. Even though they have seen the miracle-working power of Jesus, they can't seem to apply that to this particular storm. So, they come screaming, "Jesus, wake up. We're going to drown."

First He takes care of the storm, and then He asks, "Where is your faith?" He says that to them several times in the Gospels. He is probing them. He's probably thinking, *If these guys don't get more faith than this, they're not going to make it*. He sees one of their weaknesses as little faith, so He keeps addressing the soft spot that could bring them down.

There is something in every teenager that will one day make him or her crash unless it is dealt with. In fact, we are all fatally flawed, and on the devil's great big strategy map in hell, he's got a big red spot over our weak areas. He's going to aim the flaming arrows toward the holes in the armor.

Our job as disciplers is to find and confront in a teenager the thing that could trip him up. We win the right to do that by expressing that we really believe in him. If he has felt affirmed by his youth worker about his strong points, then that adult has a right to say, "Scott, I think you know by now I believe in you and your potential. I've told you that and tried to show you. Well, I have to tell you something to be honest with you, and I'm going to do for you what I wish somebody had done for me. There's one thing that I think one day might trip you up. And, Scott, if you ever want me to tell you what that one area of concern is, ask me and I'll be glad to."

It's great to try to get him to ask for it. At that point, it's an open door to say, "I think the one area that you sometimes have a problem with is authority." Or "I think one day your tendency to get angry when you don't get your way is going to wipe you out." Or "The way you handle commitment is shaky. Jesus said, 'Let your "yes" be "yes" and your "no" be "no."' Well, sometimes your 'yes' turns out to be a 'no.'" Gently approach a teenager saying, "I think the one thing that's holding you back from being everything I believe you could be is this . . . ."

That teenager needs to know that you're there, willing to work together with him on that area of his life and look in the Bible for answers, if he wants you to. He needs to hear, "You're too good to ruin. You're too good to crash. You've got too much of a contribution to make and I think the devil is going to try to stop you one day, and he might use this weak area. Let's work on it. If you've got a fort, you want to close up the hole in the wall. That's the one place they're going to get in. We're going to do it."

Give Them Responsibility

The fifth and final step in the process of discipling is to *give them responsibility*. There are several examples of that in the Gospels, but a good one is in Luke 9:12–17, where the feeding of the five thousand occurs. Jesus does not need the twelve disciples to pull off this miracle. If He can make one lunch go to five thousand people, He doesn't need these guys. But notice how He approaches it. The disciples come to Him and say, "Lord, we've got a problem. No caterers and a big crowd. What are we going to do?"

Jesus says, "I agree, we do have a problem. Why don't you give them something to eat?" What a great response. He doesn't say, "I'll take care of it." He says, "Find something for them to eat."

So they go out and find this poor little kid who brought a couple of fish sandwiches from home. He's got a little boy's appetite, and this isn't even enough for him. Suddenly, there's this big guy standing over him saying, "I want your lunch." The little boy is thinking, *So do I.* Then he realizes this is a disciple standing there saying, "Jesus wants it."

The disciples can't do the miracle, but Jesus does have the disciples do what they can. So they obtain a lunch, then He says, "Sit them in groups of fifty." He gets them involved in getting the resources, then He gets them involved in organizing for the miracle. After they organize the people, then He gives it to them to hand out. Jesus could have made the food appear in people's hands, but He gives the disciples responsibility. So Peter is handing out food wondering, *Where did all of this come from?*

Jesus trained them and then gave them responsibility by giving them food to hand out. Granting teenagers responsibility is a key to the discipling process. Yes, they need to understand, and go where their discipler goes, but along the way, they need to be given increasing areas of responsibility.

There is an awesome power in trusting teenagers. When they know an adult trusts them, they'll rise to that trust. I encourage parents to say to their kids, "Here's what I believe is the right decision, but I trust you." Young people respond to trust more than regimentation.

I remember a personal example of trusting a teenager that was a real breakthrough in the life of a tough guy. One night I gave him my car keys to simply move my car in the driveway. That seemed to be no big deal. Well, this guy had been in some trouble, so he was not trusted by many adults. The night I gave him my car keys, and trusted him in a small way, did something to him.

Since young people respond to trust, it's good to let them know something is expected of them. Our teenagers are under-challenged—but they can get a glimpse of what they could be as their youth leader expects the best of them and trusts them with jobs and assignments.

NO GREATER JOY

Recently my children gave me a plaque that proclaims a verse they know is precious to me. It expresses the greatest joy of the apostle John's life . . . of my life . . . of the lives of people pouring their lives into young people. "I have no greater joy than to hear that my children are walking in the truth" (3 John 4). For my biological children and for my spiritual children, that is the great prayer of my heart. I know it is the ultimate outcome you as a developer of young lives want to see. Not to have them just believing in truth, but walking in it. Living it. Having beliefs that change their behavior forever. Discipling—done as Jesus did it—will give them the opportunity to see *you* walk in truth, then hold their hands as *they* start doing it. When your investment matures into a changed-life disciple of Jesus Christ, you will know it was worth it. John was right. There is no greater joy.

9

THE AGENDA FOR DISCIPLING

When you walk into an ice cream store, you are barraged with six zillion flavors to choose from. The girl behind the counter wants to help you in your moment of overchoice paralysis. She hands you a little plastic spoon and asks, "Would you like to taste it?" Over and over again, that taste has convinced me I wanted a lot more of what I had tasted.

In a sense, the discipling of a young person is the process of providing a taste of following Jesus, praying it will make him or her want a lot more of it . . . will make that teenager want a lifetime of discipleship. Spiritual tasting needs to be coupled with spiritual accountability. There has to be a time when young people come back and talk about what they did with what they learned. Who ever studied algebra until he knew there would be an exam? Who ever cleaned her room before she knew important company was coming? Kids act at those moments, because someone will be checking up on what they have done. Spiritual growth is accelerated in a climate where someone cares if you are progressing or not. As we begin to launch "Project Disciple," we will be using the dynamic duo of *spiritual tasting* and *spiritual accountability* each step of the way.

In order to guide young people into real discipleship, we need to know our agenda: Exactly what do we want them to grasp about following Christ? Then, what could we ask them to do that would give them a taste of this truth? In the previous chapter, we pursued the *process* of discipling young believers. The next step is to clearly define our objectives in their lives over these next few months with them.

SPECIFIC TARGETS IN THE LIFE OF A YOUNG PERSON

The agenda for discipling involves *six specific targets in the life of a young person*. These targets are the same for any adult being discipled—living the Christian life requires the same kind of discipling for any person.

Learning to Be Changed Through the Bible

The first specific target is *learning to be changed daily through the Bible*. That does not merely mean learning to *read* the Bible. What is the difference between the two? Accountability and knowing, then doing. In fact, the discipling process can be put into pretty simple words: Learn it; do it; talk about it. It is like a chemical equation:

$$\textbf{Learn it} \longrightarrow \textbf{Do it} \longrightarrow \textbf{Talk about it}$$

With this first target, we want a young person to learn how to pick up the Bible and be changed by what he reads. James chapter one calls it "looking in the mirror." Maybe as a discipling lesson one week, a teenager might study something that talks about the Word of God, like James 1:22–25 or Psalm 119.

Another week, a youth worker could tell teenagers, "I'm going to give you each a notebook. I want you to write down all seven days this week what you're studying in the book of James. We're all going to work on James, myself included. We're going to write down two things each day: (1) What did I read? and (2) What am I going to do differently because of reading it? Bring your notebook next week, and let's talk about it."

When they come back next week, some of the kids will not have done it, some did it for a day, and others did it for seven days. There are things to be learned from each of those situations, by a youth worker simply asking, "Those of you who didn't do it, why didn't you? We can learn from that." Instead of condemning a young person, make the most of learning from that moment.

Others in the group can be addressed, "Some of you started and stopped. OK, how can we deal with that, so that those seven days will not be a microcosm of the rest of your life?" The ones who kept it going, why did they keep it going?

Teenagers need to be learning, doing, and talking about it, so a youth worker should help them learn to be changed daily through the Bible. If someone told me, "Ron, you can't have six targets. You can only have one," I would have this one, because eventually a person would figure out the other targets. Young people simply need encouragement to read the Bible in order to change. "Where are we going to go today, Lord? What do You want to work on today?" That is specific lordship.

If we can develop a young man or woman who is able to daily pick up this Book, is motivated to do it, and looks for a specific act of obedience, he or she can go anywhere and remain strong. This young person could be sent to a university where she is the only Christian in the dorm. He could be sent to army boot camp or a deserted island and he will make it as a Christian. How? Because the one thing a person has to have is a lordship relationship with Jesus where He expresses His demands through this Book. One of the great keys to the Christian life is to be changed daily through the Bible.

Learning to Get Things Done by Praying

Here's the second target: *learn to get things done by praying.* This is not just to learn to pray, but to learn to get things done by praying. Young people need to know two things about prayer in order to have this kind of bold, aggressive praying. First, they need to know *who they're with* when they're praying.

When we pray, do we realize that we are in the throne room from which the entire universe is governed? Scientists have discovered a hundred million galaxies. When we pray, we are in the throne room from which those hundred million galaxies are governed, talking to the One who runs them, who invites us in Hebrews 4:16 to come for all that He has and point it at our little moment of need.

Once people know who they are with when they pray, there should only be one thing overwhelming in their lives, and that should be Jesus. Once we understand the size of who we're with, nothing else is as overwhelming.

The second thing to understand while praying is the *resources* available. When we talk with Jesus, we need to know we can aim His power at one person or one situation on earth. That's what prayer does. Prayer aims the power that runs the galaxies at one little point on earth.

How do we get teenagers to taste that? Most kids already

know about prayer, but if they know it and have learned it, now they need to do it and talk about it. They could be tapping into the power source found in our amazing God.

Maybe this is a good time to have them write a letter to God. That could be their project one week, then they come back and talk about their letter to God.

Another week a youth leader can pass out 3 x 5 cards to all the kids in the group and say, "Write down your name and phone number, then write down something so big in your life right now that only God could do it, not God with human help, only God. I want you to get in groups of twos, exchange cards, and then pray for each other's so-big-only-God-could-do-it thing." After they have prayed, ask them, "How many of you are willing to keep that card and pray for it for the next two weeks for your friend? Great. You also have that friend's phone number, so you can call and pray with him or check up on what difference your prayer may be making. We're going to come back together in two weeks and talk about what happens."

Two weeks later, it is important to learn from each prayer situation—the ones where nothing happened, and what were answers to prayer. God says "Yes," "No," and "Wait" to prayers. Some of those teenagers will see that things actually changed. When people are praying consistently for two weeks things are bound to change.

This isn't the only project that could be done. The point is: What could a youth leader have young people do that will give them a taste of the power of prayer?

Learning to Look for Jesus in the Church

The third target is to *learn to look for Jesus in the church*. If teenagers are going to be equipped to live a whole life of following Christ, then they have to know how to grow from church and from being together with God's people.

Since the early days of the church in Acts 2 and 4, Christians have become strong by fellowship with other believers. Maybe one week, the group could study what God says about the church, dealing with Hebrews 10:25, which instructs us not to "give up meeting together, as some are in the habit of doing" and perhaps including some other things on worship. What does it mean to worship Him in spirit and in truth (John 4)? There are all kinds of things to study, but how can we get them to taste it?

Here is a somewhat novel example. It would be great to tell teenagers that this week the whole group will sit in the first five rows at church, then ask them to take notes on the sermon. At the end of the sermon, have them write down one thing: "What am I going to do differently this week because of something I heard?"

It's important to stress with young people that getting something out of church doesn't start when the sermon begins. Maybe a line of a hymn or song will impact them. It's a great tasting exercise to encourage teenagers to go in looking for Jesus somewhere in the church service that day.

Learning to Recognize and Use Their Spiritual Strengths

Here's the fourth target: *learning to recognize and use their spiritual strengths.* Young people need to know what their M.A.D. (Make A Difference) equipment is. God has equipped every teenager in a youth group with make-a-difference equipment. Each has some abilities, strengths, and gifts that God wired him with to make a difference on this planet. The job of a caring adult is to hold up a mirror and help him see that equipment. For example, a youth leader can tell a teenager, "Did you know you're a leader?" He'll wonder, *I am?* He needs to hear an adult say, "Yeah, I see that when you do something, two or three other people start doing it. I don't know where you're taking them, but you're a leader. When you're doing something, people follow." Maybe that adult could tell another teenager, "Did you know you are a tremendous encourager? You have the ability to help lift up somebody who's feeling down." She will think, *I do?*

It's eye-opening and affirming to help a young person see his or her make-a-difference equipment. It might be a smile, musical ability, or radar for picking up other people's feelings. Many teenagers feel they have no gifts or talents, because they're not basketball stars, beauty queens, or straight-A students, so they need help seeing their strengths.

Part of discipling is to constantly affirm a young person's gifts. Also help the young people to start looking for gifts and talents in each other. It's great when you can get them into a group and begin to have them point out each other's strengths.

How can young people continue to taste what their spiritual strengths are? A youth leader can tell them, "This next week, every morning specifically pray, 'Lord, I dedicate my encouragement ability to you, and I want to use it in someone's life today. I'm going to be looking for a place to use that encouragement, that mercy, that leadership, that smile, whatever it is. I'm going to be looking for a place to use it for Jesus seven days this week.'"

A teenager can then record in his diary how that exercise goes each day. Next week talk about ways God used each person as the young people consciously gave back to Him the thing He gave them to make a difference. Through this they're tasting, learning, knowing, and doing.

Learning to Look for Natural Opportunities to Talk About Christ

The fifth target is *learning to look for natural opportunities to talk about Christ*. That doesn't mean just go out and witness; it means to look for natural opportunities. Colossians 4:3–4 describes Paul's prayer, as the great evangelist says, "Pray for us, too, that God may open a door for our message, so that we may proclaim the mystery of Christ. . . . Pray that I may proclaim it clearly, as I should."

One week perhaps the discussion can deal with witnessing. Here's the mission. Every week is like mission impossible, except this is mission *possible*. The mission is to pray this prayer every morning for the next seven days, and then fasten their seat belts. This is a dynamite prayer, so people should be careful, because it might get answered. It's based on Colossians 4:3–4.

Here's the prayer: "Lord, please give me a *natural opportunity* to talk about You, where it won't be walking up to someone and saying 'Turn or burn,' but a *natural opportunity* in a conversation where I can talk about You. Give me an open door."

The second part of this prayer asks God, "Help me *recognize* the opportunity when it comes." And the third part of the prayer: "Give me the *courage* to take the opportunity when I recognize it."

It's exciting to challenge teenagers to pray that prayer for the next seven days and be open to the Lord answering it. When an answer comes along, they can believe that God opened the door, and then they should look for a natural way to speak of their relationship with Jesus with that person.

It's important for young people to get a taste of a natural opportunity to tell about Christ. One of the reasons we don't know about this is because we don't go looking for opportunities. For one week, it's great to get them looking for natural opportunities. It could change their lives, and they could end up living their whole lives like that.

Learning to Behave Unselfishly in Personal Relationships

The final target is: *learning to behave unselfishly in personal relationships.* That's about a perfect description of a Christlike lifestyle, putting other people first instead of yourself. Living in sin means "me first," but living like Christ wants us to live means "others first."

Maybe one week the group could study John 13, the foot-washing passage. Yes, that's a nice Bible story about Jesus washing feet, but do those teenagers really believe the story? They're probably thinking, *Yeah, I believe that. That's good.* Then suddenly their youth leader says, "Let's go wash some feet this week."

Then he or she can say, "I have good news for you—you won't have to wash actual feet. But let's do the equivalent, because nowadays we don't have open sandals and dirty roads. Write down on this 3 x 5 card one job in your family that everyone hates to do. During this next week, do it without complaining—even if it's not normally your job. Don't make a big announcement; just do it. As you're doing it say, 'Lord, this is for You. I'm doing this for You. I'm doing this to learn how to be like You.' "

Another example might be for them to identify one person in their life who is a difficult person. They shouldn't call that person an enemy, but let's call the person an "unfriend" in their world. During this next week, they would pray for that person every day by name and ask God to show them a way they could express caring for that person, even if they don't feel like it, and even if their gesture is unreturned. They should do it because that's how Jesus treats people, and this next week they're going to try to treat other people like Jesus would.

Again, the following week those young people should get together and talk about it, and they should know that their youth leader is doing this too. A youth leader can tell the kids, "If I'm going to ask you to do it, I've got to do it too."

If I had one year in the life of a teenager or a small group of kids, by the end of the year I'd like to know I'd done all I could to see that they have learned how to do these things, tasted them, and talked about them. I can't change their lives; the Holy Spirit will do that, but this seems to be the process by which it is done.

SPECIFIC GOALS FOR THE DISCIPLER

In summary, the discipling approach is accomplishing *long-range spiritual objectives* through *short-term achievements.* An effective youth worker needs to have lifelong goals for the kind of Christian he hopes a teenager will be. One goal is to have him be in the Bible the rest of his life and to pray. Any discipling plan needs to give young people some short-term achievements, because they need to build some spiritual confidence and say, "Hey, this works. I could do this. The Christian life is not the impossible dream and just for older people. This is doable."

We should always have long-range spiritual objectives in mind, but those aren't for teenagers to know. We know where we're going and what we'd like them to be the rest of their lives, so we need to get them doing some short-term achievements that will give them a taste for more and give them confidence that it works.

The dream and payoff for paying the price to be a discipler is that we will produce some young men and women who will be followers of Christ and make more of a difference than we ever made in our whole lives.

What an epitaph and tribute, if we can stand before Jesus some day, as Paul said he would with the Thessalonian Christians, and say, "These are my crown of rejoicing. I don't even need a crown. They are my crown" (see 1 Thessalonians 2:19–20).

Discipling is costly, but it's worth it.

10

BUILDING AN
EFFECTIVE YOUTH GROUP

We always met in the basement and we sang a lot of choruses. That was Youth Group 1960. Of course, no one ever thought in advance about *what* choruses we might sing—so our monotone song leader punted by asking the infamous question, "Any favorites?" Yes. "Do Lord." Every week— "Do Lord." It was probably selected on the basis of its rich spiritual meaning—"Do, Lord, oh do, Lord, oh do remember me. Way beyond the blue." Who needs a speaker when you have music like that?

If we went to a second "favorite," we were almost surely into "Give me oil in my lamp, keep me burning, burning, burning . . . keep me burning till the break of day." Again, we were deeply challenged. Especially by the "creative" verses that followed—"give me gas in my Ford, keep me truckin' for the Lord" . . . "give me unction in my gumption, let me function." Once we made it through two or three more favorites, we had those ever-present announcements—and then a speaker. I always looked forward to the speaker—he meant refreshments were next. At the end, the youth group president (with only about ten kids, you were bound to be an officer sometime) would give his familiar challenge—"Bring a friend next week." Not a chance.

That was 1960—the "good old days." Our little cluster of Christian kids would be there for youth group, no matter how boring the program was. After all was said and done, just being together was probably the magnet that kept us coming. Fast forward to today—from "Sesame Street" on, today's teenagers are the products of a high-tech, high-energy, high-gloss youth culture. Many of the kids of the church would rather have their "fellowship" in the youth culture than in the youth group. Bring a friend? We would be happy if they bring *themselves*.

Yet the church youth group is more important now than it ever has been. In a world where families are dissolving, the youth group can be the support group many kids desperately need. In a world where young people are more of a separate culture than they have ever been, the youth group can be the place where the claims of Christ are translated into a teenager's world. The more pagan the society, the more essential the support group. That is why those early believers "every day . . . continued to meet together in the temple courts" (Acts 2:46). Christianity has always been a team sport. If ever that sense of not being alone was critical, it is now when a teenager's whole world seems to shout, "Who cares what God thinks?"

But "Do, Lord" in the basement won't do it anymore. Today we are *fighting* for young people, including the kids of the church. "Youth group" has to be reinvented for the needs and wavelengths of a whole new teenage world. Some basics have not changed and they never will. In other areas, today's youth leader needs fresh thinking, plowing a new path where the old "young people's group" used to sit. The church youth group is "base camp" for the Christian young people who are the frontline soldiers in the battle for their generation. It is a "field hospital" for the many wounded kids. And it must be the redeeming place where Satan's prisoners of war are attracted and set free.

ASKING THE RIGHT QUESTIONS

Too often our youth groups are characterized by apathy more than excitement, by having meetings more than making a difference. The first step in building an effective youth group has almost nothing to do with the young people themselves. It has to do with the *leaders*—and seven honest questions that ask them to look in the mirror before looking at their kids.

Are We Assuming Too Much About Our Young People?

It is easy to accept their "right answers" and assume they are much farther along spiritually than they are. Maybe they need to have a climate where it's OK for a kid to admit he is not a Christian. Many church kids have the mask, the vocabulary, and the name—but not the Savior. They need leaders who acknowledge that real possibility and provide them the freedom to admit they have missed Jesus. Or perhaps those who are Christians could "get real" in a climate where they feel that it's OK to be struggling and not know all the answers. They need a place where it's all right to admit, "Frankly, I think the Bible's boring, and I pray and nothing happens." What's not OK is to fake it. The truth is acceptable, but not masks.

Are we assuming too much about them? Maybe we need to back up and start to define the basics with our young people—which for too long we have assumed they understand.

Are We Powered by Prayer?

Is our youth ministry literally dependent on prayer? Do we have a prayer team in this church who prays whenever we're having a youth meeting? Do we have a prayer team of warriors to whom we refer names, who can keep confidences, and who are praying for those teenagers who are hard, struggling, backsliding, or considering Christ? Is prayer just something we use to open and close a meeting, or is it the power plant of our work with young people?

In the story of Moses, Aaron, and Hur, the Jews prevailed against the Amalekites as long as Moses could hold up his arms. But he couldn't keep them up all day, so Aaron and Hur walked with him and held his arms up (Exodus 17:10–12). Every youth worker needs an "Aaron and Hur club" around him or her—this is war. We cannot afford to have a ministry that is program-driven or idea-driven or even goal-driven. It must be a prayer-driven ministry, or we will only see results *humans* can produce. Fervent, focused prayer will give us what *God* can do for our young people. "The prayer of a righteous man is powerful and effective" (James 5:16).

Are We Tackling the Real Issues?

Are we tackling what teenagers feel are the issues as well as areas we know are the "invisible" issues? Are we dealing with different aspects of relationships, whether it's how to forgive someone who's hurt them, how to deal with a family that's breaking up, how to get along with parents, how to win parents' trust, how to build a no-regrets relationship with the opposite sex? Are we dealing with issues that are real to them? What about the issues we know are just as real, but under the surface? Are we teaching them about Satan and how to recognize his attacks, since he is so active these days? Are we showing them how to cope with loneliness and the mistakes people make when they're lonely? Are we confronting the area of sex and how young people can make moral choices they won't regret in two weeks or two years? In a word, is our youth ministry *relevant*? Does it connect the Word of God to the world they live in?

Do We Know Why We're Meeting?

At first, this question may sound out of line and unnecessary. But, unfortunately, the only reason some youth groups are meeting is that there has always been a youth group and meetings are what youth groups do. But someone needs to sit back objectively and assess *why* we are meeting. What's our mission? Are we aiming at nothing and hitting it? Is our activity getting us to our goal?

Are We Seeking Right Answers or Changed Lives?

It is important to remember that discipling is about changing behavior, not just learning answers. What's our goal? Right answers or changed lives? The answer will affect how we program and everything we do.

Are We Willing to Change?

If we find that we're not getting the result that we want, are we willing to stand back and say, "Maybe something needs to change. It's not working"? Change is threatening—but not nearly so risky as losing our kids to the darkness.

What Kind of Growth Are We Seeking?

Are we more concerned with the growth of the young people or the growth of the youth group?

We need to do what's best for them to grow individually, not simply what will build a bigger youth group. After all was said and done, Jesus' "youth group" ended up with eleven people—but they changed the world. Teenagers are not bodies to populate a youth group. We don't have young people so we can have a youth group. We have a youth group so we can have young people who follow Christ.

This kind of personal inventory has to precede any plans or programs. If our assumptions, motives, or modus operandi are not right, we will not "bear fruit—fruit that will last" (John 15:16). With this look in the mirror, we are ready to make a life-changing plan.

CREATING THE RIGHT STRATEGY

With those questions as a starting point, we are ready to pursue a three-step strategy for building a strong, effective youth group.

We have to first do some research and development if we want to rebuild a youth group. In a sense, there is a chance to do that each year, because every year is a new start. With a church as a whole, building tends to be continual; but with the youth group, every September offers a chance for a new beginning. So, a youth worker can stand back and say, "OK, before we head into another year, let's do our homework."

Identify Your Young People

Here are the steps in doing your homework. First, *identify your young people.* There are two groups to identify. First, identify the *"actives"*—those kids who are actively involved in the group. The goal is for the active kids to become part-owners of the church youth ministry—no longer spectators. Producers, no longer just consumers.

Fans, compared to the players, are lightweight party people. There's a guy with his beer hat and beer belly who's making noise, yelling how every play should be executed and criticizing when the team doesn't follow his advice. The players on the field have their lives, careers, and bodies on the line. Sometimes I have wanted to go up to that guy and say, "Excuse me, sir. Why don't you get out of the stands for a few minutes and get in the game? Let's see how well you do."

It's easy for teenagers to sit in the stands and say, "This youth group is boring. We're not doing much. I don't know why we should come." We need to challenge our young people to lose their fan attitudes and get in uniform—they're starting! Players on the field don't have time to complain or criticize—they're too busy playing.

After figuring out who the active kids are that can be challenged to become part-owners, the formation of a "Teen Action Council" can provide a place to get involved. The name is not important, but, whatever you call it, it ought to be a representation of all the major cliques in the youth group. Even in a small youth group, there are often two or three cliques. It's smart to get together some of the really motivated, spiritual young people *and* also some of the best of the "fringe" kids.

Ownership begins as the youth worker helps those young people start to pray by name for other teenagers. They can begin a prayer ministry for the second group in your research—the *inactives*. After focusing on the active young people, the youth leader needs to identify and make a list of the inactive kids. The inactives are those who have had some connection to the church but are MIAs (missing in action) as teenagers. Maybe they were touched by the church as children, they're relatives of someone in the church, or they used to attend Sunday school. These are the potential prospects. If you and your team do your homework, the list of inactives will most likely be longer than the list of actives. They are teenagers who at least know where the church is and have been in it sometime. So, the active young people start praying for the inactives, "Lord, help us get these kids back." The actives also need to start praying by name for non-Christian friends.

Once the actives are "on the field," the youth leader should get them involved in giving leadership in all kinds of areas. Maybe they can help with decorating a youth room—"OK, this room has been given to us. How would you guys like it to look?" Let them form a committee and make it their room. Now they start to feel ownership. (Back in our "Do, Lord" days, we had to take the church basement as it was.)

It is vital to get young people out of the mentality that they are coming to watch a show the youth leader is putting on for them. The active kids need to be elevated with the challenge that "from now on, we're all putting on this group for those young people who aren't coming yet. It's going to be yours and I'm going to help you. Me coach, you players."

A good basketball coach is usually back and forth, intense, yelling, emotional. But the one thing he cannot do is to go out and shoot a basket. He knows what the players ought to do, but he can't do it. An effective youth worker is the coach on the sidelines. The teenagers are the players. The coach cannot win the game, and kids need to know that. The youth group "actives" can be told, "I want you to realize this is a team of which I am the coach. A coach without players goes nowhere. I hope you need me as a coach, and I hope I can be a good coach. But I'm getting you guys ready to go out and play the game on your own."

What do we do about our other target group—the inactive kids? First, why are they inactive? One way we can find out is by asking them—sending out a survey, calling them, or having our active teenagers each take one or two of them and say, "Hey, you used to come. Why don't you come anymore?"

Then we need to ask, What would turn these young people on to coming? The Teen Action Council young people should be owners, not watchers, by now. Once we find out why some teenagers are inactive, how can we conquer some of that? We can ask the active kids, "Guys, what do you think? You're their age. What would help if that's their reason for not coming?"

Another question is: Who from our active teenagers knows them best? Divide up the inactive kids among the actives, according to who knows each one best.

When it comes to a meeting location, could the group meet at the house of someone who hasn't come for a long time? What if the group had a pizza party at the home of one of the inactive teenagers? It's good to go to their turf and see if they will host something. Chances are, some of their friends will come if the event is at their house. And the friends probably will not be the kids you are used to seeing.

Any effective strategizing for your youth ministry needs to first identify your young people, the actives who need to become owners and the inactives who need to be the reborn mission of the youth group.

Identify Their Needs

The second step in doing your homework is to *identify their needs*. An effective youth worker realizes that life-changing youth ministry is *need-oriented*, beginning where teenagers are. The starting point is a list of the *felt* needs of the teenagers in the group. The "actives" leadership group could help with answering the statement: "This youth group would be worth it if you could help me or help my friends . . ." The answers could be written down on a blackboard or flip chart, because an up-front listing evokes more response. The leader will already know some of the young people's felt needs, but he will probably learn some new ones through having the active kids help.

It's also good to identify the *invisible* needs—needs that you as a leader may know the young people have but they don't know they have. For example, they might not put on the list, "I need to know how to get something out of the Bible," but you know they need that. It's important to figure out a way to get to those invisible but real needs.

After identifying their needs, those needs can be converted into subjects for meetings. That's what I do with the radio program, "Alive!" Every program starts with a need that is developed into a broadcast. Then, it's good to look around for resources that can help tackle that subject. Is there a video on it? What Bible passages deal with this need? What speakers deal with it? What Christian songs are about this need? The whole equation starts with identifying your target teenagers, then their needs, then youth group subjects that will meet those needs along with resources that can help.

Identify the Purpose of the Group

The third step in doing your homework is to *identify the purpose*. Why is this group meeting? "Fellowship" is probably an inadequate answer. Is the main purpose of a youth group to sit or to serve? To have meetings or to make a difference? A mission will drive a youth group to be a living place. Instead of wondering "what kind of meeting they're going to have for me this week," teenagers start asking, "What kind of a difference can we make?"

If a church has a group of young people who are dead in the water, maybe the youth worker should decide that for three months, they won't have any meetings. At that point, it might be better to get some of those teenagers to go out and try to meet some needs in the community. Instead of sitting around, they can get a taste of being in the game. A time-out in the week-after-week schedule can help break the cycle of apathy.

One youth group I know of came alive in a great way. Because of the leader's and kids' gifts, they formed a youth choir and got excited about doing some contemporary music. They needed a drummer, but the only drummer they could find was not a Christian—so in came unchurched Rich. Before long he came to Christ and is now in ministry. Their reason for getting together was to build a youth choir, not just to have a youth group. But each time, before they practiced, they had a Bible study. And the study didn't feel like study for study's sake—it was preparation to make a difference.

A youth leader from New England told me, "Our youth group has had about twelve kids doing nothing. Once I took two of them with me to a rescue mission in downtown Boston." Like a good discipler, he took them where he was going. He continued, "After we left the mission, they said to me that they really liked doing that, and asked to go again sometime." This was the first time he ever saw them interested in something, and it was like they suddenly woke up.

On the next visit to the rescue mission, a couple more teenagers went along. Pretty soon all twelve of his kids were going. He said, "Ron, now our youth group has about fifty kids. That mission became a reason for us to be, a reason for us to know, a reason for us to study, a reason for us to learn. We had a reason to exist that was bigger than us."

A rescue mission is one example of a place for teenagers to make a difference. Locally, there might be a senior citizens' home where there's a building full of lonely people. If some teenagers went to it on a regular basis and read to them, listened to them tell their stories for the fourteenth time, sang to them on their birthdays, and remembered holidays, the kids could light up the lives of those lonely people. Young people would begin to say, "Hey, I can make a difference." Basically, we're giving teenagers a game to get involved with before continued "practices" or meetings. But now, they have a reason *for* the practices—so they can get ready for the game.

The same dynamic happens on a missions trip, when a leader takes a spiritually "blah" teenager to another country or into a needy place in the United States. In our own country, there are enormous needs on Native American reservations, in the inner city, and perhaps in your own town. Young people from wealthy suburbs can go and tutor little kids in educationally impoverished urban neighborhoods. Teenagers can go to Haiti, the Dominican Republic, Mexico, Europe, the former Soviet Union, or anywhere, and it's amazing what happens to them. There is a world out there to reach for Jesus, and young people learn that they can do something about it.

When teenagers are in a place where the money, language, and food are foreign, suddenly they're reading their Bibles at seven in the morning. Many kids have never before read their Bible in the morning, but now they feel they need to. They're in a situation where they're teaching a Vacation Bible School or building a church, so they begin getting into God's Word.

Some teenagers start praying out loud who had never done

so back home. Other kids ask, "How would you tell someone about Christ?" They now have the need to know, because they're not sitting, they're serving. A mission motivates them to learn the information necessary to be a Christian and to meet the needs of others. Young people come alive spiritually in a situation where they're beyond their resources, asking, "What do you do for a lonely, ninety-year-old lady? For this homeless man? For this exchange student who is so far from her home?"

Luke 12:48 says, "From everyone who has been given much, much will be demanded." The biblical principle is if a person has a lot of something and someone else has a little, the first person should give some of his to the second person so they both have enough. Finally, teenagers have some people who need them and they're outside of themselves, depending on the only person who can help them in that situation, Jesus Christ.

I believe so strongly in getting kids involved this way that if I were able, I'd get every teenager on a missions trip. A youth pastor's wife once told me that their youth group took some food and clothes to the homeless in New York City. She said, "It was amazing, because the kids who got into the project the most were the 'fringe' kids. The teenagers who usually hung around on the fringes of our group, and who didn't really participate during meetings were the ones going down in the subways trying to find homeless people, and on the front lines handing out blankets. It was a wake-up call to them—they had a purpose. There was a reason to exist other than 'Do another meeting for me.'" Miracles happen when teenagers have a mission.

The purpose for a group should be mission oriented. Of course, the teaching of God's Word must always be central to powerful youth ministry—but teaching brought to life by *doing* God's Word. James 1:22 is virtually a battle plan for life-changing youth ministry—"Do not merely listen to the word, and so deceive yourselves. Do what it says." When young people are exercising spiritually, their leader will notice an exciting difference when he feeds them spiritually—they will have an appetite.

Identify the Resources

The final step in the homework process is for a youth leader to *identify the resources*. This involves shopping around for any local resources that could be used. Where are Christian musicians who could be brought in? Who in the local area can talk about a specific issue? What movies and videos are available? It's a good move to get some Christian catalogs and match them up with the needs that have been identified in that group: "This video addresses this need. This movie deals with this need." Where are some special spots in the area to take them? What would be some good trip locations within an hour or two?

By doing his or her homework before plunging into youth ministry, a caring adult is paying the price for spiritual success. It all begins by identifying the young people you want to target . . . then the needs that drive their lives . . . the mission purpose that will awaken your young people . . . and finally the resources that will address their needs. Doing your homework gives you what you need to move into the needy lives of young people—a map to go by.

CREATING THE RIGHT CLIMATE

In youth ministry, climate is primary and program is secondary. Ultimately what will get and keep teenagers is the way the group feels, not the circus that is put on every week.

Certainly, there is no excuse for mediocrity in programming. Today's young people are used to excellence in programs. But if we had to choose between making teenagers feel loved and important or putting on a dazzling show, the caring should far outweigh the programming. That's exciting, because that qualifies many more people for youth ministry—there are more people who care than there are showmen.

If the climate of a youth group is decisive, we need to explore the elements in a climate that will attract and keep young people.

Caring Leaders

I was once told by some young people, "We don't think our youth pastor really cares about us. We're not sure he likes us that much."

I asked, "Why do you say that?"

One young man replied, "Well, he puts on good meetings, but he's gone within ten minutes of the time the meeting's over."

I don't think they ever told their youth pastor that, but they were getting the message he didn't care. They didn't remember the program, because the program didn't say "I care about you." They wanted him around, to be the last one to leave. He was a veteran in professional youth ministry, but he failed the most important test kids give us—the caring test.

When I train volunteers to work in a youth ministry I say, "The first question to ask yourself is: Do you have the ability to make a teenager feel important? If you have that ability, you can have a great ministry with young people." Ultimately, it is making young people feel loved that will open all kinds of doors into their lives.

The Right Time and Place

The second ingredient that contributes to the climate is *the right time and place for your meetings*. We need to be asking what time and place would help young people be the most relaxed, the most open, the most likely to come, and the most likely to bring their friends.

It might even mean moving the youth group out of the church. It's important to remember here that we're not concerned about the youth group; we're worried about the young people. Not all the youth meetings need to be held in the church building if it turns out to be a less effective setting. Do we need to meet in homes? Do we need to meet in a school? Do we need to meet at some other neutral place? The meeting place is not sacred—the ministry is.

What is the best time for teenagers to come? Is it Friday night, Saturday morning, Sunday night, a weeknight? All options need to be open.

Attractive Packaging

Teenagers will get a message about whether or not this program is going to be quality from the publicity that promotes it. There is probably someone in every area who could never lead a Bible study for young people, but they sure could do great publicity and a great mailing to them. Those are valuable adults to get involved—the people who are sitting around in every church who think there isn't anything they have that the Lord could use, but they could do a cartoon or a clever mailing. By sending out a regular mailing that's attractive and fun, you will communicate that this is a program teenagers can trust. Posters, publicity, and mailings are all part of the packaging.

Another important part of packaging in the climate is *music*. Teenagers love music, so it sets a "something's happening here" tone when kids walk into a room where music is playing. Music also provides a "touch of class" as background for slides, games, and refreshments. It is a powerful energizer.

More Teenagers

Young people like to be where there are other teenagers. They may be bored with their youth group because there are only eight kids and they're sick of seeing those seven other faces. The antidote is to occasionally combine with some other small groups to create more energy and excitement by moving out of our little cocoons.

The identity that is most important to young people is not what youth group they're in but what school they attend. That's where they "live"—Central High School. So, we need to start to get all the Christians from Central High School knowing each other, even if they're in six youth groups.

Variety

Another ingredient in the climate is *variety*. The meeting should not be the same week after week. You can change location, format, emcee, media—the point is not to provide the sleeping pill of predictability. There are many programming helps out there to do that, especially at Christian bookstores.

Informality

Informality should characterize the climate of a youth meeting. A youth group should not just be mini-church. Food helps make a climate more informal—so it's good to have pizza, cookies, something to drink, or something fun to eat, because people are different when they're eating. It's like when adults meet over a cup of coffee. Something about having a cup of coffee or eating relaxes people. Maybe that is why Jesus so often broke bread with people.

Daniel had a burden for the young people in his church—both of them. I met Daniel after he participated in an "Alive!" youth broadcast radio taping. He was from a little town in Iowa, and he told me, "We had two kids in our church—there was really no youth group. We didn't know what to do, so we would eat pizza and get together each Saturday night to listen to your 'Alive!' radio program. Afterwards, we would talk about whatever you discussed on the program. That's all I knew to do."

He said, "Soon those kids brought a couple of friends and now we have a group of twenty. We don't always listen to the program, but I always tape it, and later we'll sit down, listen to it, and then talk about it."

That's an informal get-together that worked for a guy with a heart. He didn't have much of a plan, and no training, but the youth group increased in size ten times!

A Family Feeling

Teenagers are looking for a sense of closeness and intimacy. One way to have a sense of family is by praying together. Young people need to see that when someone has a problem, it's prayed about.

Also, it's thoughtful to have a group do things to remember each other. Teenagers will want to be part of a group where if one person is hurting, everyone does something about it. So if there are twelve teenagers in a youth group and one is in the hospital, he knows that he'll get cards or a visit from eleven people who care. Or if someone misses school, it's good to know that a friend from youth group cares enough to call and say, "I missed you. Where were you?"

It's exciting to find ways that a group can reach out and care for one another. Of course, the way they'll get the closest is by working together for the Lord. People never get close by having a lecture on closeness. People who are closest to each other are those in combat together, making a difference together—people who have a common cause.

During the Vietnam War, there was a TV special about a southern, black sergeant who commanded a unit made up of southern whites and a few other black soldiers. Against all the odds of their backgrounds, tremendous bonds developed between these men. The documentary was called, "Same Mud, Same Blood." Those men were fighting a common enemy, and suddenly the differences between them didn't matter any more.

The greatest clique breaker in the world is a mission young people do together. Mission will unite and excite people. Teenagers need to be doing things for the Lord together. Unfortunately, an annual missions trip isn't enough—they need a local mission. It bonds kids when they go to the same nursing home together, help the same hurting people together, walk through the same needy neighborhood together. That is how a youth group becomes a combat unit instead of just people who hear war stories. And "going to battle" together will build in them those close family feelings young hearts crave so deeply.

WORKING YOUR PLAN

After you do your homework and create a climate, it is time to work your plan. That plan needs to include several interest-building, life-changing elements.

Image-Building Events

Many youth groups have an "image" problem—they are presumed to be small and unexciting. Some larger, high-energy events can help change the "boring" perceptions that keep young people away.

It all begins with a kickoff event that communicates, "This is going to be a year too exciting to miss!" It's important to make sure a lot of the "inactives" are at events like these. Tell them, "If you don't like it, don't ever come again. But you have to try it one time."

Have a great time that night, with a little music. Maybe throw in a video and say, "Here are ten things we're going to do this year. We want you to be in on these experiences. We hope you'll be back next week. If you would like us to mail you regular information on our upcoming events, give me your name and address tonight." No big spiritual agenda this time—just an activity that feels great, quits while you're ahead, and briefly explains that, in the midst of the good times, you will be exploring the difference our Creator can make in our everyday lives.

An attractive retreat is also a good kickoff and image-builder. At any image-builder, it always adds a lot to have slides or videos of teenagers up on a screen, because they love to see themselves up front. To get photos or footage, simply go over to the local school, and if some of the teenagers in the youth group, including "inactive" ones, play a sport or are in some activity, take pictures and then give them a place to see themselves. These image-building events are to get some excitement generated to get some energy going from a dead start. Teenagers want to be where the action is. Image-building events serve notice that *this* is where the action is.

A Creative Format

A creative format is an important element in your plan. For example, role plays involve the group and provide an alternative to a lecture format. If the topic is family relationships, the teenagers can be their parents and the youth worker be the teenager. Then everyone can talk about the role play, how they felt about how the parents handled it, etc. Role plays bring them into an issue.

Discussions also vary the format. Surveys are one way to help jump-start some teenage talking. A youth leader can throw out a sentence like, "I most fear . . ." A little written survey on "I most fear" can help generate input from a silent group. Halloween is a good time to do a survey asking "What do you fear the most?" If teenagers don't volunteer their answers themselves, someone can read some responses anonymously, and then ask the group, "What do you think about that? How do you feel about this one? How many of you have ever felt that way?" Surveys are a creative way to sometimes break up a meeting format.

Practical Content

Third, *practical content* is needed in your youth group plan. When preparing for ministry with young people, there are two key questions to always answer when speaking: "How?" is the first. We cannot give them "shoulds" without "hows." Remember, we leave kids stranded in "should-land" if we do not also show them practical ways to implement what they should do.

"So what?" is the other question our presentation needs to answer. It will help us prepare wisely if we imagine that at the end of the presentation, each teenager will hold up a card that says, "I agree, so what?" Inside, they're probably thinking, *So I agree that it's true. So what do you want me to do?* When a speaker answers the "how?" and the "so what?" questions, he has provided young people with the kind of practical content that changes lives instead of merely filling heads.

Follow Through and Feedback

Finally, *follow through and feedback* are part of an effective youth ministry plan. Some kind of feedback device, like the reaction card mentioned earlier, completes the communication process. It is always important to get feedback from teenagers about what was discussed that night. Then follow through is the point at which action projects are presented—the kind of Christian life projects described earlier in the agenda for discipling. Your young people take the truth that has been taught and put it to work during the week in a spiritual "action lab." The following week those real life "so what?" experiences become the subject of a sharing time. This makes a youth ministry an active growing process for a young person rather than a passive learning process.

Follow through and feedback encourage response, interaction, and connectedness—all valuable contributors to making truth come to life.

Model Vision

A living youth group can give life beyond its own circle. Young people have the power to model what the whole church could be like. Instilling a "make a difference" mind-set in teenagers includes challenging them with a vision for their own church. The seeds can be planted by asking youth group teenagers to finish statements such as: "I wish our church was more . . ." and "I wish our church was less . . ." "I think we could be 'make-a-difference people' for this church if we . . ." They need to see that *they* are the church, too—and that together they can make their part of the church what they would like the whole church to be. Or in the inspired words of the apostle Paul, "Don't let anyone look down on you because you are young, but *set an example* for the believers in speech, in life, in love, in faith and in purity" (1 Timothy 4:12, italics added).

A leader with a Jesus-heart will challenge the young people to be what they would like the church to become. Teenagers can catch a vision that says, "If it starts here, maybe it could spread throughout the church."

Christian young people need to realize their potential to be spiritual examples for their church and beyond. They could be God's instruments to lead the church into something more loving, more evangelistic, more exciting, more real than many adult believers are experiencing.

After all, a lot of them have sat around a campfire singing, "It only takes a spark to get a fire going." They could be that spark.

11

BUILDING RELATIONSHIPS WITH TEENAGERS

Tissue boxes have pictures of beautiful flowers all over them—even though flowers have almost nothing to do with blowing your nose. Cereal boxes display famous athletes and goofy cartoon characters who have nothing to do with frosted corn flakes or little oat O's. Frozen dinners picture what's inside as rich, succulent entrees—but sometimes provide a meal that tastes only slightly better than the container it came in.

It's all about packaging. Anyone with something to sell knows that the package may very well determine our response to a product.

When the "product" is the love and life of Jesus Christ, the package is just as important. In one sense, exciting programs and publicity create a "package" that helps attract young people to Jesus-places. But for two thousand years, the essential package of the Gospel message has been something far more valuable and effective—a person. Ultimately, the package that advertises Jesus most powerfully is a person who is like Him.

Nowhere is that more true than with today's young people. Their real search is for love, for understanding, for significance. No program can give them that. Only a person can. In the end, it will not be the adult who can tell the best jokes or shoot the most baskets who has a life-changing youth ministry. It will be the adult who can get close to teenagers and provide the caring they are starved for. But the trick is that "getting close" part. How can an adult go about building a quality relationship with a teenager?

A relationship is vital in connecting a young person with Jesus. Teenagers want to see if the thing this person talks about really works. They evaluate the truth of what a person tells them in the context of a relationship with that individual. The most powerful platform for reaching teenagers is through a relationship, not a meeting or being up front with a spotlight and microphone.

There are two dimensions to changing a teenager's life. There is *the sharing side*, where someone shares the message; and there is *the caring side*. One is basically doing, and the other involves just being with them.

An effective youth worker cannot choose one or the other. Either caring or sharing comes more naturally, easily, and instinctively for each person's personality. With some people, the relationship side is easy—it's not too tough to care, love, express interest, comfort, ask questions, and pray with someone. But sometimes those people find it difficult to let the deeds proceed from caring for someone to presenting Christian truth to that person, and then asking for life-change.

Other people are the opposite, and they have no problem with the proclamation part. They're motivated to get God's truth into people's lives, but the caring side is harder to do. They want to get to the point right away.

Usually, ministry will demand that a person grow in one area or the other. Youth workers cannot simply say, "I'm more comfortable caring, so I won't do much sharing," or "I'm more comfortable sharing, so I'll let someone else care." To be a life-changing agent in young people's lives, it's important to learn how to both care and share, because, biblically, both are needed.

For many of us, it seems almost intimidating to try to get inside a teenager's life. Teenagers do not open up readily, maybe because they have been hurt or neglected too often. They do not seem to be looking for an adult to trust—some have simply given up believing there is such a person. But if a make-a-difference adult will make the effort to pursue an authentic relationship, he or she will find the keys to unlock a teenager's soul. At the least, caring adults can give young people a tangible taste of how Jesus feels about them.

BRIDGING THE GAP

Once when I spoke at a conference located on Lake Michigan, my son and I went off to climb a giant sand dune. By the time we finished, it was hot and we were tired, so we looked for a short-cut back to camp. We thought we had discovered a shortcut when we found ourselves by the edge of the water, at the shortest point between the camp and us. Well, the camp was in sight, and that was where we wanted to be to cool off and rest, but we couldn't get there because there was no bridge across the water. We thought for sure there would be a bridge somewhere on this shortcut, but we ended up having to go back the long way around. We saw our goal, but there was no bridge.

Relating to young people today grows more difficult with every birthday we have. A wider and wider gap continues to grow between adults and teenagers, yet teenagers are an urgent mission field. We may think, "There are the kids I want to reach. They're right over there. I'm motivated to reach them, but how do I con-nect with them? I need a bridge." Here are ten ways to construct a bridge into a teenager's life—to build a life-changing relationship.

Follow the Leader

First, we need to *follow the Leader,* and have confidence knowing that the Divine Matchmaker is directing us to young peo-ple we can help with what we know. We must trust Him, because He knows what we know and He knows who needs that, and He is good at bringing people together with the teenagers who they can best help.

This divine matchmaking happened over and over in the Bible. Philip was suddenly told to leave his evangelistic meetings, and the Divine Leader matched him up with a fellow from Ethiopia.

Ananias was having a nice quiet day, when God came in and almost ruined his day by saying, "I've got someone I'd like you to go talk to."

Ananias asked, "Who, Lord?"

God said, "Saul of Tarsus."

Ananias said, "I'm a dead man."

God simply said, "Trust Me. Go see Saul." Ananias didn't want to go, but he did, because he trusted the Divine Matchmaker.

God was constantly directing people in the Bible to these divine encounters. If a person today is a prayed-up missionary, he or she can assume that God will match him or her with the appro-priate young people. That adult can walk with a confidence that is not based on how cool he or she is or how responsive those teenagers are, but on the sovereign leading of the Holy Spirit, bringing lives together for God's glory.

As people follow the Leader into the youth culture, a neighborhood, a school, their own church, there is an important prayer to remember: "Lord, guide me to the teenagers that You want me to relate to." We need to pray before we go, pray as we go, and pray after we've been there.

As chairman of the Northern New Jersey Billy Graham Crusade in late 1991, I heard of an amazing matchup that occurred after an invitation to know Christ. Thousands of people flooded forward to come to Jesus, and one of the trained counselors was looking and praying for the person God wanted him to match up with to counsel and lead to Christ. God led him to stand behind a certain man. When Billy Graham asked everyone to match up with a counselor, the man turned around, saw the counselor, and asked, "Don't I know you?" Sure enough, the man counseling and the man coming to Christ that night had done drugs together several years earlier, and they hadn't seen each other since.

In a sea of thousands of people, how could any counseling supervisor on earth ever organize that kind of matchup? Only the Counseling Supervisor in heaven could match those two together! That is the same sovereign Holy Spirit who is leading all of our lives, unless we're ministering on our own steam. If we're trying to minister to others in the flesh, forget it. But if we are praying daily through our contact with people, we can assume the sovereign leadership of the Holy Spirit and relax knowing the Leader is in control. He is the One "who directs you in the way you should go" (Isaiah 48:17).

Take the Initiative

The second step in relationship-building is: *Take the initiative.* An individual may feel insecure with a young person, but the person needs to realize that teenagers feel even more insecure with an adult. Young people may act arrogant, like they have it all together, or like they don't need anyone, but any adult is far more secure than teenagers are.

An adult needs to make the move and be prepared to go 80 percent of the way to have a relationship with a teenager. Anyone who is looking for a fifty-fifty relationship will probably not have many relationships with teenagers.

The youth worker should not expect much initial response from a teenager. Most young people do not know how to respond to an adult who wants to be with them and get to know them. One of the skills that any person needs to develop when relating with young people is the ability to talk about nothing. Yes, we have the ultimate Someone to talk about with them, but with kids, we need to be prepared to pay the price of some small talk in order to win the right to have some big talk. There's a lot of small talk in school—talk about boyfriends and girlfriends, what was on TV last night, what game or concert is coming up, and who's having the party. To us, it may seem unimportant, but it's not to them. After we wade through some of that, eventually the time comes when we're able to turn the corner to something more significant.

Also, usually it is easier to meet teenagers individually than with their group. They are harder with their group than they are alone. Most teenagers are different people when you meet them without their "audience" around. In a group situation, suddenly coolness and toughness take over. An adult will do much better if he can find a moment when that teenager is alone.

It is also important not to try too hard and to be yourself. After all, God thought you were the one who should do this job. If a person is in His calling and His will, He doesn't want them to become someone other who than they are. There are plenty of teenagers who need someone like *you*, not your copy of someone else.

You do not have to become a teenager to meet a teenager. It's better to be a secure adult and not go in to impress them. If a person's idea is to impress young people and let them know he or she is important, kids will pick that up and go the other way. Instead, an adult should let a teenager know that he or she is important as a young person.

An obvious part of taking the initiative is to go into a teenager's world to meet them, as Jesus came to ours. We cannot wait until they come to our world—we need to be at their practice, rehearsal, game, concert, or something that matters to them. When we show up someplace we don't have to be, it shows we care. We have to be at our own meeting, so that doesn't show we care. It's when we go to *their* meeting that they sense our interest in them.

When you show up at a teenager's important place, you shouldn't expect the young person to embrace you and verbalize how happy he is that you came. The teenager won't say that the "I care" message got across, but he quietly marked you "present" in the mental scorebook. If we look for feedback, young people will disappoint us. We need to be prepared for a predominantly one-way communication for a while. No response does not mean no impact.

If you put your self-worth in the hands of a sixteen year old, he or she will most likely drop it and probably step on it several times. So, you have to know who you are and not derive your worth from young people you work with. We're there to help them with their worth and their needs, not vice versa.

One way to take a social initiative is to ask for their help. For example, it's easy to ask them for information when going to a game or something, like "Which way is the field?" or "What time's the game?" Meeting someone is easy when simply asking for information. You might even ask a teenager to take you where you need to go. While walking along, you can ask your guide if he knows so and so. Bridges can be built by putting yourself in situations where you need them.

It's also smart to keep your eyes open for little clues you can use as conversation starters with teenagers. For example, look at what a teenager is wearing. Does he have the name of a music group or a sports team on his shirt? "Oh, so you're a Yankees fan, huh? Have you been to a game recently?"

One door-opening approach is to ask the question, "How's it going?" and mean it. Usually people don't listen for an answer when they ask someone how it's going—so it doesn't take much to stand out. Look them in the eye and listen to how they're doing. Follow up on their answer by asking, "Really?" and usually people respond with a different answer, because they can tell you really do care how they are doing.

In an insecure, uncaring, cold world, it is the missionary who must take the meeting initiative. Don't wait for teenagers to come to you. Even if you have to go 80 or 90 percent of the way with them, you won't be going as far as Jesus did to start a relationship with us.

Express Interest in Them

A third way to build a bridge to another generation is to *express interest*. First, you need to ask what the main areas are in a teenager's life. That provides a mental menu from which to order some get-acquainted questions. They have a family, grades, teachers, work, friends, activities—and all of these can be either good or bad in their eyes.

You can ask, "How many are in your family?" or "Oh, you're

the youngest; what's it like to be the baby in your family?" or "What's your favorite subject in school?" or anything about the basic arenas of their life. If the teenager is in a sport, there are obvious questions to ask: "How is the team doing? How's the year going so far?" It's good to keep in mind a mental checklist of things that young people are interested in and then draw on those to ask some interesting questions.

While you are listening to a young person, listen for something that can be pursued further. When he says, "My dad doesn't live with us anymore," later you might ask, "You mentioned your dad doesn't live with you. How long has it been that way? Since you were twelve? How did you feel about that at the time? How do you feel about it now?" It opens more conversations when you follow up on things someone has briefly mentioned in answers to questions.

Sometimes it's hard to find something a quiet or shy teenager is interested in. I once knew a quiet teenager named Joe, and I was trying to figure out how to get into this guy's life. Every door I knocked on was a dead end. Finally, one night I asked Joe, "When you're feeling something real deeply, how do you express it? Do you ever write anything down?"

He said, "Oh, yeah."

I said, "You do? What do you write?"

He said, "Oh, I write some poems."

Open door! I said, "Really? Would you mind if I saw them?"

He asked, "You want to?"

I said, "Sure, if they're expressing what's going on inside of you, I'd love to read what you wrote."

Next week, he came back to our meeting with a book full of poems. It took a little while to find his interest, because it wasn't sports, student leadership, or any really typical activity. We need to keep probing until we find their key. It could be their favorite music group, who they hang around with, their boyfriend or girlfriend, or their job. Maybe they write or sing. There is a key to every life. As long as we keep expressing interest, we'll find that key, and when we do find it, we need to express a lot of interest.

A highly-trained Christian counselor I know once had a pretty tough case. Some parents had brought their sullen teenage son in for some help. The son said, "My parents made me be here, but you aren't going to get anything out of me." The counselor tried all the conventional things to get into the problem area of the kid, but the guy sat staring at the floor for the first forty minutes of the session. There was no response.

Finally, the counselor went over and lay down on the floor underneath the guy so he could look him in the eye. Then he observed, "You brought a magazine with you. What is it?"

The guy said, "It's just a motorcycle magazine."

The counselor asked, "Are you into motorcycles?"

"Yeah," said the guy. For the last twenty minutes of the session, they talked about motorcycles. They didn't talk about dysfunction, they simply discussed how a motorcycle functions.

The next session was the two of them riding the motorcycle. They didn't do any counseling at all. Well, there was a counseling breakthrough several weeks later. How? The adult counselor expressed interest in the teenage boy's world. He found one area of interest with that young man and pursued it. There is an old saying, "Love me, love my dog." In this case it was love me, love my motorcycle. Other teenagers are saying love me, love my sport, my poems, my concert. Caring adults should take an interest, even if it is something they may not like all that much.

I spoke with a veteran youth leader who is now a grandfather and pretty far removed from teenagers. He blazed some trails in youth ministry years ago, but today he doesn't have a chance to be around many teenagers. However, he has teenage grandchildren.

He told me that while speaking to his granddaughter one day, she said, "Grandpa, my favorite music is Guns & Roses." He wasn't quite sure who that was, but he knew it probably wasn't real good. She said, "Of course, you would hate them."

He said, "Well, I don't know. I haven't heard them."

She said, "No, you wouldn't like them at all, Grandpa."

He said, "Well, you talk about them all the time, so let me listen to them."

"You want to listen to them?" she asked.

"Yes. Do you have a recent album?" he asked. She was sure that he would be upset about what he heard and condemn her. True, he wasn't happy about much of what he heard.

Later, she asked him, "What did you think, Grandpa?"

He responded, "Well, I kind of like the third cut on the second side. The way they approached the subject was interesting." He won over his granddaughter at that point, and he also won the right to have an opinion about her music, because he had listened to it, shown respect for it, and looked for what he could like in it.

He won his way into her heart by taking an interest in something that he didn't even really approve of. He probably expressed to her some of his concerns, too, but first he took an interest in what interested her. Being interested in someone is within the reach of anyone who tries.

Focus on Them

A relationship begins to grow with a young person when you *focus on him or her*. When you are with a teenager, act as if he or she is the only person on this planet.

Few people have the ability to make someone feel as if he or she is the only one around. These exceptional listeners don't look across the room, wave at anyone else, or look at their watch. Instead, they fully focus on a person while they talk with him or her. That's a tremendous ability, and it makes people feel important.

When focusing on a person, be like a camera that focuses on one face or one object in a crowd. Mentally put your lens on one person, focus on him or her, let the background fade into a blur, and act like there's only one person in the world right then.

Missionary and martyr Jim Elliot said, "Wherever you are, be all there." That's the biblical principle of wholeheartedness. Whatever you do, do it with all your heart. When you're with a person, be with him with all your heart, and don't be with anyone else. That teenager is all that matters at that moment.

Jesus had an amazing ability to do that. There was always a crowd of people surging around Him, and they all wanted a piece of Him. He was approached one day by a lady who had been bleeding for twelve years. She was out of money and out of hope, but she knew if she could grab Jesus' garment she would be OK. She lunged for Jesus and touched His garment—and He asked, "Who touched Me?" The disciples responded in words something like these: "What? Who touched You? A thousand people touched You." But Jesus knew exactly who that one desperate woman was in that surging crowd of people (see Luke 8:40–48).

Jesus was able in the middle of a crowd to feel the needs of one person. The more you become like your Savior, the more you will become like that.

You may not drive the coolest thing on four wheels, may not dress with this year's hot jeans or sneakers, and may not be real clever with a punch line, but all of that doesn't go very far. It might help open a door, but it doesn't say, "I love you and care about you."

Of course, focusing on someone also means remembering that person's name. So, usually it's good to not meet too many people at once, or there will be a barrage of names to remember. People love to hear their names. Teenagers often say, if and when I can address them personally, "I can't believe that you remembered my name." What helps name amnesia is to use a teenager's name as soon as you hear it—several times if possible—and then to think of some unique way to remember it. After you leave a teenager, pray for that person by name . . . and keep praying for him. As you do, he will begin to become part of your heart.

Another way to focus on teenagers is to be with that person or group in your mind even before you're with them in person. For example, are they in the middle of final exams right now, is school vacation coming, or was there some crisis in that teen's life? By entering their world, you're ready to talk with them, because you've been mentally joining them in their world.

Affirm Them

Another step in building a relationship with a teenager is to *affirm that young person* by telling him what you like about him. It's helpful to look for strong points to compliment, because most kids receive little praise in their life.

If a young person's parents are focused on performance or themselves, that son or daughter doesn't get much praise from mom or dad. He or she probably just hears about the "bad" things, so he or she doesn't know what he or she is doing right. If she has a great smile, tell her. If he is generous, tell him. If he shows leadership ability, tell him.

Some of us adults would personally be much farther along in our own lives if more people had affirmed us earlier in life. Some of us are still trying to figure out what our strong points are, because we were never told. God didn't create anyone without some make-a-difference strengths, but we find them out when people hold up a mirror. In the Bible, God often changed people's names to reflect who they were. Abram became Abraham, and Sarai became Sarah, which means "princess." Barnabas's real name is Joseph, but the disciples said he was a real encourager, so they changed his name. What did Barnabas do the rest of his life? He lived up to his name, encouraging those around him. How about Simon, the unstable flake? Jesus said, "You're now going to be Peter, the rock." Peter, Mr. Up and Down, Mr. Emotional, became a rock in Jesus' eyes, and he lived up to it.

Part of the mission of a caring adult can be to help change the names of some teenagers they know. Most kids have been called some destructive names, like Stupid, Ugly, or Loser. The wounds from names go deep and last for years in people's lives. But God beautifully renames people. There's a great ministry of calling people by a new name and saying, "You're an encourager. You're a giver. You're a leader." If we help "rename" some people like God does, many of them will probably have a tendency to live up to their new names, like people did in the Bible.

Sea World has a show where dolphins do tricks and then get a fish reward from their trainer. If someone will give a dolphin a fish, he'll jump through another hoop. People are like that too. Whatever someone gives them a fish for, they will do again. When someone gets a compliment, he or she will tend to do that same thing again. When a teenager is called by a new name, he or she may do more of the thing you affirmed in him or her. God believes in rebuilding people by calling them new names—so should His ambassadors in youth ministry.

One way to affirm teenagers, and also meet them, is to look for some young people who have done something noteworthy and send them a note. I once was trying to meet the quarterback of a local high school football team, and I didn't quite know how to break into his life. After a great game he had one week, I jotted him a little note, saying, "Dear Tom, You've made a lot of us proud of you and given the school a lot to be excited about. I appreciate the price you're paying to be the leader of the team that you are." He might have vaguely known who I was, but we had never talked. A couple of weeks later, I was there as the guys were coming off the field. Here came Tom all muddy at the end of the game. He saw me and said, "Hey, thanks for the note."

A note in the life of a teenager is an event. For someone to go out of his way to write a thank-you note says a lot to a teenager. Or a leader can say, "Thanks for the comments you made at the meeting last week; I think they helped a lot. They gave me a lot of insight. Thanks for taking time to help me understand." Affirming someone is a strong opener for a relationship.

Serve Them

Another step along the road to a relationship with a teenager is to *serve him*. The Bible does not say, "We do not preach ourselves, but Jesus Christ as Lord, and ourselves as your *leaders* for Jesus' sake." It says, "your *servants* for Jesus' sake" (2 Corinthians 4:5, italics added). That's a great motto for someone in youth ministry.

What are some practical ways to serve teenagers? Give them a free ride. Until kids get their license, they're always needing a ride somewhere. Help tutor a student in whatever subject he is having a tough time with. Help coach a teenager on certain sports techniques for free. Serving the young people you meet is a *mindset* more than a list of ideas. If you have a "what can I *do* for this young person?" outlook, the ideas will come naturally.

Learn from Them

Learn from that young person—that is an effective way to take your relationship to the next level. As we've mentioned, it presents a great opportunity, when we put ourselves in a situation where we're willing to not know about something they know about, whether it's a music group, a car, or a sport. If they know we don't know something, they would love to tell us, if we would let them. It's great to get under the hood of a car with a young person who knows all about cars, and let him or her explain to us what all those things are underneath. We'll be winning a friend, because we gave them the dignity of teaching us.

Trust Them

A teenager responds when you *trust him*. When getting to know a teenager more and more, it is wise to appeal to our trust in him or her as a motivator. Something positive happens when you say, "I believe that you're going to make a right decision in this situation. I trust you. Here's what God says about it. Here's what my experience is with it. I've told you what the advantages and disadvantages are. I trust and respect your right to make this decision." Trust significantly deepens a relationship.

If a teenager betrays trust, it's OK to tell the person in an uncondemning way that you need and want to be able to trust him or her. For example, you might say, "Those calls to other kids needed to be made, and I thought you would do that. I just have to let you know that I feel a little let down that you didn't." Kids need to know that you want to believe in them, that you are in their fan club. They need to know that you believe in their strengths and that it's important for people to be able to trust them. It's also wise to tell a young person to let you know if you ever let him or her down. Trust goes far in a relationship with young people.

Challenge Them

Another deepening step in your relationship with young people is to *challenge them*. We cannot build a relationship at the expense of the truth. People who are instinctive relaters sometimes tend to compromise the truth, because they're afraid the truth will compromise their relationship. The biblical model out of the book of Ephesians is "speaking the truth in love" (Ephesians 4:15). When you confront a problem, you need to include love with it. Often, the "truth-ers," who are real good at giving the truth, aren't very loving. And the lovers sacrifice the truth for love. Biblically, a person cannot sacrifice either one. We should say, "I love you enough to tell you the truth." Then keep on showing love, even if that person rejects the truth. It's important to always wrap the truth in love.

In a relationship with a teenager, it's necessary to have some backbone and not sympathize with his sin. We need to care, but to affirm or condone something we know is wrong is misguided love.

For example, it's really easy to oversympathize with a teenager when he talks negatively about his parents. But ultimately, a caring youth leader has to come down on the biblical side of honoring a father and mother or he has departed from our orders. We cannot depart from divine revelation in order to better relate with a young person. Teenagers need the truth about what God says. Expressing sympathy for their feelings is fine, but not sympathy for their sin.

It is more important to be respected than to be liked. In fact, Jesus wasn't liked by everyone, but no matter how His enemies probed His life, they could find nothing wrong with it. They had to invent charges to crucify Him. He was respected even by His enemies.

We do a teenager no favor if we sacrifice the truth to keep a relationship. Youth workers cannot be moral pushovers. They do need to be prepared to say, "I can't agree with you on that. I understand why you feel that way, and I respect your right to make your own choice. I'll be your friend whatever you choose, but you need to know what the Bible says about this. I wouldn't be your friend if I didn't tell you."

An effective youth worker will have some backbone in a relationship, and not just be a soft, pliable person. Many of the elements in a relationship with a young person emphasize gentleness and tenderness. But love sometimes has to be tough love—not rejecting love, but love that does not lower the standard. On the other hand, we should not come across as judgmental when we are taking a stand for what is right. When we present God's truth, confrontation must be without condemnation. When we speak the truth in love, a person should feel more valuable, not less valuable . . . cared about, not condemned.

Don't Disappoint Them

The final "how" in building a relationship with a young person is actually a caution: *Don't disappoint him.* As a caring adult, it's important to keep your word, promises, and commitments whether he does or not. Be on time whether he's on time or not. Keep your end of the deal, and always be credible. If he shares a secret, keep his confidence. What will kill someone in youth ministry faster than anything is for word to get out that a youth leader told a confidence of another person.

When you are trusted with a confidence from a person, he or she has probably looked through his or her life and said, "I don't know whose hands to put this in, but I think I can trust you. It has taken me a long time to trust, but I'm going to put my life in your hands right now." That is not something to dare pass around, even as a seemingly innocent "prayer request."

One of the weaknesses of some people in youth ministry is that many of us are insecure people down deep inside. One way to build ourselves up is to brag "spiritually" about the young people we've counseled and say, "I was dealing with Margaret about suicide this week. It was neat the way the Lord worked in her life." That sounds spiritual, but it is also self-promoting.

It dignifies no one to divulge a confidence. By breaking a confidence, a person says to everyone that he or she cannot be trusted. People will make a mental note to not share something with that person in the difficult times.

Credibility is so key in not disappointing someone. Proverbs 22:1 says, "A good name is more desirable than great riches." It's important to not do anything that would cost credibility with a teenager. Promises are a big part of that credibility—and they should be made carefully. It's easy to make a casual promise that will make a teenager feel good right now, "Yeah, sure, I'll call you later." The leader may forget; the teenager won't.

You lose nothing by not making a promise, but you lose a

great deal if you promise something and then don't deliver. So, when you make a promise to a teenager, it's important to move what needs to be moved and bend what has to be bent to keep that promise. The price tag for broken promises is broken relationships.

THE GIVING OF ME

If teenagers had plenty of love and adults who cared, it might not be so critical to invest in a relationship with them. But they are victims of a relationship famine. An adult who cares enough to take the risks of relationship-building can bring so much hope, so much worth into a young person's life. There is no more compelling package for the Gospel of Jesus Christ than an adult who will wrap that truth in a relationship. Someone in a famine will open the door to a person who is bringing something to fill the hole in his stomach. Starved for caring, a teenager will open his life-door to someone who offers love to fill the hole in his heart.

The apostle Paul understood the personal investment required to have a life-changing ministry. He summarized it in a letter to what was perhaps his fastest-growing, most fruitful church. He says, "We loved you so much that we were delighted to share with you not only the gospel of God but our lives as well" (1 Thessalonians 2:8).

"I shared the gospel of God." That is where the power is to change lives. Yet Paul seems to say, "I didn't just give you my talk and my message, I gave you me." "Not only the gospel of God, but our lives as well." If you want to eternally impact young lives, you will have to be willing to give them your message . . . and to give them *you*. Like Jesus did for us.

12

WAKING THE SLEEPING WARRIORS

My wife and I love to grab a weekend in Pennsylvania Dutch country. This charming Amish area is a peaceful, scenic place to visit—and a great place to eat. Several restaurants offer unforgettable home-cooked, family-style meals. One of our special places is called "Good & Plenty," and it deserves the name. A dozen people are seated at each table, and the waitresses bring out huge platters with roast beef, chicken, potatoes, fresh vegetables, homemade bread, and more. The only way to justify eating this mountain of food is to starve yourself all day, maybe all week.

Unfortunately, there was a slight malfunction the last time we ate there—not with the restaurant, but with the guests. One couple seated at the end of our table served themselves, then kept all the food at their end, chowing down while forgetting all the other hungry people down the table. So, here was this mountain of food piling up at one end of the table, while the rest of us sat at the other end with empty plates. A few people stuffing, most of the people starving.

Sadly, that is an all too accurate picture of many American Christian teenagers. They have tons of Christian goodies piled up on their plates. There's a mountain of "food," made up of meetings, concerts, camps, retreats, music, and more. While most of their peers are starving spiritually, they are piling on another helping.

Never has a generation of young people in the history of the Christian church been so rich. Past generations probably couldn't even imagine the wealth of resources the American church has today, and much of the rest of today's world doesn't comprehend it at all. They cannot conceive of the endless banquet of Christian activities and resources we enjoy.

Luke 12:48 says, "From everyone who has been given much, much will be demanded." In fact, that is true of the whole American church. We are the richest Christians in church history, and our kids are certainly "overblessed." Those of us who are involved in the lives of Christian young people have the responsibility to challenge them with the job they need to be doing. The reason they are bored is that they have eaten so much that they're stuffed. It looked good when they first started to eat, but when people kept telling them to eat more and more, they got sick of their Christian diet. We need to help them step out of their own boredom and do something with what they know. They are terribly underchallenged.

If a teenager is not challenged, he will be bored; there is nothing in between. Spiritually, we cannot allow our young people to simply have a piled plate while others starve. We'll get bored with our own ministry, and they'll get bored with our ministry unless we challenge them. When young people are actively making a difference, their faith is no longer boring.

Our Christian young people are God's sleeping warriors, and they are overdue for a wake-up call. They are the frontline troops in the battle for a generation, but they don't know it. It is our assignment as leaders to sound that wake-up call.

One of the hindrances that will keep us from waking up young people is the Lone Ranger complex. The Lone Ranger is a good idea for a western hero, but not as a style of youth ministry. Some of us tend to be do-it-myself type of people. Instead of empowering the young people in our churches, too many youth leaders want to be spiritual heroes reaching as many young people as they can alone. Instead, we need to empower, enable, and motivate an army of evangelists. We cannot do the job ourselves, so we need to recruit and help train an army.

An effective wake-up call to the youth group's sleeping warriors must offer them two strong motivators. First . . .

A MISSION THEY CAN OWN

If fellowship is the only reason for getting together, that is not challenging enough. Their goal should not be survival, playing defense—but playing offense spiritually. It is time that young people have a mission they can own, marching under the banner, "We can make a difference!"

In high school, one of my sons was active in a local prayer breakfast where kids gathered once a week near their school and prayed by name for their friends and for God to move on their campus. Many of these prayer breakfasts began to spring up around northern New Jersey, and they even saw teenagers come to Christ at those times of prayer. It is exciting to see a tremendous, rapidly growing prayer movement of young people across this country. Some young people are praying regularly in prayer triplets, where three Christian people get together and pray for three non-Christians each. Regularly, nine unbelieving friends are being prayed for. When we have had prayer triplets organized through the "Alive!" radio broadcast, we called them the "transformers."

Transformers are those gray boxes that hang on telephone poles near homes. They take all the millions of volts of power in the wires near the street and bring that power down to a level where it's useful in our homes. That's what prayer does. Teenage "transformers" are bringing millions of spiritual volts of God's power from the throne room of heaven, right down to one friend they're praying for that day.

A *prayer breakfast* or a *prayer triplet* is a mission teenagers can easily own. Preferably, a prayer triplet should be accountable to an adult. That adult doesn't necessarily check up on the teenagers, but he or she should be available when needed. He or she can also help coordinate a prayer breakfast where all the prayer triplets can get together. The point is that there's a person who cares that young people are praying, asks how it's going, and helps enable them.

The growing youth prayer movement surfaces most dramatically at "See You at the Pole." This historic prayer mobilization happens annually when groups of Christian young people get together and pray at the same time on the same day in September, around their school flagpoles. This movement has spread rapidly across the nation. Many teenagers get together, join hands, and pray for their campus, the teachers, and their friends. Some precious kids are all alone when they pray at the pole.

It's good for any youth group to know that there is a movement of prayer growing and that they're missing something if they're not involved. They don't have to start it, because it's already started. That's the way they can begin to taste a mission they can own. It's a bite-sized mission, and it's affecting their world.

Another mission a teenager can own is an *equal access club*.

This club, which can have any creative name, is based on the equal access laws that say a student-led initiative with a faculty sponsor cannot be forbidden in a public school unless all extracurricular clubs are forbidden. It is only legal if it is student-led. There are various materials available from different ministries about how a teenager can organize such a club.

I once heard about a soldier who took artillery classes in the army years ago. He reported that everyone was bored in class . . . until they were about to be shipped to Vietnam. Suddenly everyone was taking notes, asking questions, staying after class. Same subject; same material. Boring before; interesting now. The difference? They were headed into a battle where they were going to need that information.

That's what Christian teenagers need. They need a battle where they're going to need all the things they're being taught. Their battle is a mission they can own.

Make-a-difference youth leaders need to think through how they can give young people a mission of their own. Some of that involves a mission to their school, but there are other needs in their community as well. Ruth was a teenage gal I knew who was pretty depressed much of the time. I once told her she had a caring spirit and encouraged her to visit the local senior citizens' home. Soon she was visiting there a couple of times a week, and now she's a doctor. Once she got a mission, she finally got outside herself and found some people who needed her. It was amazing to see how it cured her problems of self-pity, loneliness, and lack of self-worth. Those elderly people were a mission she could own. I don't know if she changed their lives. I do know they changed hers.

There is a second motivator we can give to God's sleeping warriors. We can give them . . .

A VEHICLE THEY CAN TRUST

No, not a reliable set of wheels. They need an *outreach* vehicle they can trust. They need to own a mission, but their youth worker needs to give them an evangelistic vehicle—a meeting, group, etc.—that will always be the kind of event they can bring a lost friend to without embarrassment. It's important to have a consistent, quality outreach program that young people can trust.

A youth worker needs to always be prepared for whatever meeting he or she has, and make sure it always has style, using the principles of programming that were mentioned earlier. It needs to be an attractive vehicle that a teenager can talk to friends about and invite them to. Even if the friend isn't interested in going to a youth group meeting, most young people are interested in a pizza feast night, or the world's largest pillow fight, or a make-your-own video night.

When you offer a social hook, you have given your Christian teenagers something that's easy to invite a friend to. It may even mean doing attractive programs for several months when teenagers don't bring their friends, because they're just beginning to trust in the program themselves.

After awhile those teenagers will begin to get confident enough that they'll bring a friend to the vehicle their youth director has provided. They need to hear from their leader, "Guys, there are things you can do for lost kids that I can't do. And maybe there are a few things I can do that you can't do. I can train you in how to get your mission done, but I can't do your mission. That school is your mission, not mine. You don't have the time to put together a regular program, but I do as part of my job. I guarantee that if you'll accept the responsibility for your friends, I will give you some tools to work with that will help you reach them. I'll try to never let you down with this. You be there with your friends, and I'll be there with the tools you need to reach them."

That is the kind of battle plan that can get the sleeping warriors onto the battlefield—and their friends to heaven! Ultimately, the wake-up strategy must present young believers with the two weapons they will need before they will be willing and able to fight.

THE "WANT TO"

All the training in the world will make no difference without the motivation to put it to work. Before we can equip our young people, we have to motivate them to care about making a difference. In order to have a "want to" for ministry, Christian kids first must see . . .

The Battle Raging

They need help standing back and seeing what's going on with their generation. They need to know that right before their eyes Satan is working overtime to produce a generation where the lost kids know nothing about Jesus and the found kids aren't living for Him—a generation he can finally own with his death and darkness.

We leaders must help our Christian young people realize that

God has chosen them to live in this generation, where the battle has grown more intense. God has chosen them to be on the front lines of the most important days of the battle. We can tell today's young people, "We already know who has the winning power in this battle. The only way we'll lose is if you don't show up or if you surrender."

I like to ask young believers some questions and let their answers make a revealing point. First question: "Do the kids at school who drink a lot keep it a secret?" They almost always reply, "No, every Monday morning, people are talking about the weekend and who got the most wasted." I ask, "Are the people who have sex keeping that a secret?" Most teenagers say that both guys and girls brag about their sexual experiences, to let everyone know they've done it.

I always close by saying to them, "Well, isn't it interesting that the people who are talking are the people who are ruining their lives. It seems like the good guys aren't talking at school. The only people talking are those who are in the darkness on a dead-end street. The people making noise are those on the street going nowhere." I have been excited to see them respond to a challenge that says, "We've got something to talk about, but we're not. They've got nothing to talk about and they're bragging. There's a battle raging right there at our school, in our neighborhood. Do we want to desert or fight?"

The Urgent Need

In addition to seeing the battle raging, young believers need to see the urgent need of their friends. Let them know that most people who ever accept Jesus Christ do so by the age of eighteen. Paint a picture for them saying, "When you go to your graduation, most of your friends who graduate without Christ will probably live and die without Him. We don't get another chance with most of them. Now is the most urgent time in their life." Eternity is hard to see from the walls of high school, so teenagers often need our help glimpsing the urgency of sharing Christ with their friends in these few short years. With the sense of urgency, Christian young people should be able to see . . .

The Responsibility

"No adult can go where you go, or be as close to your friends as you are"—that is the challenge our kids desperately need to hear. For Christian teenagers, it is a case of "If not us, who? If not now, when?" If they introduce a friend to Christ, they have instantly changed that friend's eternal address. They have in their hands the power to help fill the hole in a friend's heart and change a life for all eternity. But they are not in this alone—God is on their side, giving them the words and the courage their mission will require.

A battle raging . . . an urgent need . . . an eternal responsibility—when a leader can give his young believers this kind of look at God's big picture, he or she has provided powerful "want to's" for making a big difference. Armed with the "want to," teenagers are ready for the other weapon they will need in the battle.

THE "HOW TO"

Once a teenager is motivated to help get a friend to go to heaven with him, that motivation will die if he doesn't know the "how to." Basically, there is a "tale of three people" that explains the "how to" of their divine assignment. Three people make up this life-changing, make-a-difference transaction. The three people are (1) a Friend to tell about, (2) a friend to tell it to, and (3) a friend to do the telling.

A Friend to Tell About

Their message is a *relationship*. They're telling about a *person*, not a religion. They are not trying to sign up their friends for Christian beliefs, a religion, or a group. A teen is telling a friend, "I have found the relationship we're all looking for. I've got to tell you about who it is." All they have to do is tell about the most important relationship in their life.

We need to say to Christian teenagers, "You don't have to be a theological expert, go to seminary, or know fifty Bible verses. Simply tell your friend that you know Jesus, and what that relationship is like. It is a *person* you're telling about. It's Jesus. Remember that Jesus said, 'Follow Me.' Jesus said to follow Him, not His followers, leaders, nuns, priests, or pastors. Jesus is the issue."

It is liberating for young believers to realize that their message is ultimately a Friend to tell about. There are a couple of wonderful examples of this in the New Testament. In John 1:41, Andrew instinctively knows what he needs to do as soon as he comes to know Christ; he runs to tell someone else about his decision. Andrew goes to his brother Simon, but he doesn't say, "We have found a new religion." No, Andrew says, "We have found the Messiah." They had found a Person.

Then, in John 4, the woman of Samaria did not invite her fellow villagers to "Come, join a religion." She urged them to "Come see a *man* who told me everything I ever did." She had found a person. She said, "I don't know a lot about this, but what I can tell you is there is a man you have to meet." That kind of "you ought to check out Jesus" witness was doable for that woman who had just met Him. It is certainly within the reach of any Christian teenager.

I love the example provided by the blind man Jesus healed (John 9). His testimony was not, "Once I was blind, but now I have joined the Christian faith. Once I was blind but now I have a new belief system." The blind man simply reported what had happened to him—"I was blind, but now I see." One reason so many Christians remain silent is that they fear questions will be raised that they cannot answer. But once we understand that our message is a Person and His impact on our lives, we are free to say, "I can't answer all of your theological questions. . . . I just know that I was blind, but now I see. And I'll tell you who healed me."

"Witnessing" has been encumbered with some unnecessary fears. Telling of Christ is simply that—and a good youth leader will uncomplicate the mission by making that clear. Chapter 6 presents one method for explaining the Gospel that youth leaders can teach their kids.

Part of equipping our young people to tell about Jesus is to help them build their testimony. Most teenagers probably have no idea what their testimony is, so they can't talk about the difference this relationship makes. To help change that, I give kids a form to fill out that has three horizontal sections on it. The paper is called "The Story Only I Can Tell." While sharing about Jesus with someone, there are really two stories a person is telling—His story and their story. His story is the Gospel, and their story is the difference Jesus has made in their life. Their story is the story only they can tell.

The top section of "The Story Only I Can Tell" is marked, "B.C.—Before Christ"; the middle section is called, "The Turning Point"; and the bottom section says, "A.D.—Since Christ." Each section has space for someone to write. B.C. is where I write about the me that existed before Christ. The turning point is where I put a description of how I came to Jesus. A.D. is the description of my life since Christ came into my life, and the difference He is making.

THE STORY ONLY I CAN TELL

B.C.—Before Christ

_____

The Turning Point

_____

A.D.—Since Christ

_____

Usually that form is easier for teenagers to fill out who remember what "lost" was like. What about those kids who grew up in a Christian environment, who don't know what testimony they have? Here is a statement that those teenagers can finish, that gives their testimony: "If it weren't for Jesus . . ." or "If there were no Jesus . . . ." If there were no Jesus what would their lives be like? Have them write briefly on that topic—how would their lives be different? What wouldn't they have that they do have now? What would be missing?

How would it be different for them and their family, their loneliness, their problems, or their fears? It's important for young people to know what their testimony is, so they know how to easily tell a friend what difference Jesus makes in their life. Jesus is the Friend to tell about; He's person number one in the tale of three people.

As we help young believers realize Who (not what) their message really is, we need to remind them that the Jesus story is the ultimate love story. This One they tell about loves them and their friends beyond description. At a recent camp, a street-hardened young man came up to talk with me after I spoke, his eyes welling with tears. He said, "I want to talk about that relationship with Jesus." When I asked him why, he answered softly, "Because no one ever loved me like that. No one ever loved me enough to *die* for me!" It is that awesome love that ultimately must cause a Christian teenager to say, "I cannot be quiet about my Jesus any longer. I cannot let my friends go any longer without knowing the One who loved them enough to die for them." *How* does a Christian teenager begin to make a difference? First, by realizing he or she has an incredible Friend to tell about.

The next step in understanding their mission focuses on the second person in this tale of three people . . .

A Friend to Tell It to

Instead of saying, "OK, I'm going to go and reach my school," a teenager needs to get a burden with a name. To help kids focus on a lost friend, I have often asked them to make a list of four names—"four friends of yours that you don't think are going to heaven right now, who you most want to have there with you."

After that, I tell them, "You can't have four, only three can go. Which one are you going to cross off?" So, they cross one off their list. We do that two more times until they're down to one. Then I say, "You can keep one. You are looking at the name of the person you most want to see in heaven with you. Here's the big question—what are you going to do to get him or her there?"

Challenging teenagers to step up to the responsibility for one friend is a doable starting point for a personal mission. Maybe eventually they'll get to the other three that were on their lists and many others, but right now, the point is to focus on one. It might seem as if sharing Christ with only one friend is pretty limited. But one friend is probably one person more than they have ever witnessed to. This "target teen" gives a focus to their burden and a name to their spiritual responsibility.

This should include focused prayer, too—"Lord, I'm praying for Kim again today. She's going through it right now," or, "Lord, please bring something into Tom's life today that will give me an open door and a chance to talk to him." Praying by name for someone will give focus to their prayers. And once they have seen one of their friends come to Christ, it's habit-forming. They'll be off and running as witnesses for Christ.

One haunting question has to be dealt with before most kids will share Christ with their friends—"How do I start?" Basically, this is much like when parents talk with their children about sex. Instead of having one big "birds and bees talk," it is better to have a process of explaining things in regular conversation. When talking with someone about Jesus, there is an unfolding process involved. It isn't one big "Jesus talk." During regular conversation simple things can be said, such as, "I prayed about this" or "Can I pray for you right now? I'd love to pray with you."

Praying with someone is a simple, compelling way to bring up Jesus. People are intrigued when someone prays with them. I have had many unbelievers express appreciation, because they were glad to know I was praying for them. This can best be done privately or on the phone. Praying with someone demonstrates the relationship a believer is trying to present. When someone prays with a friend, he or she is having a relationship with God in front of that friend. It is one of the simplest ways to get started.

Another way for someone to get started sharing Christ is through a *crisis* in his or her own life or a crisis in the friend's life. That provides a wonderful opportunity to tell about the difference Christ can make. If a "tell it to" friend is going through a hurting time, the Christian teenager can step up as that friend's "be there" person, prayerfully looking for a natural open door to introduce

Jesus' love. If the young believer is the one in the crisis, he needs to see the opportunity it offers, not just the pain it is causing. All approaches to life work when things are going well. The test is when the bottom drops out. For a Christian, this is the golden moment to show the Jesus-difference.

Another opener is *lending a friend a book, magazine, tape, or CD*, or something that presents Christ and has meant something to him or her personally. It is better to *lend* than to give, because when that teenager gets it back, he or she has the opportunity to ask, "What did you think?"

Of course, a teenager should also invite a friend to a *Christian activity*—but not just depend on the Christian activity to reach them. This is where the leader is responsible to provide a vehicle that teenagers can trust and feel confident inviting a friend to. Our young believers can be encouraged to talk to their friends after the meeting and say, "What did you think about what the speaker said? What do you think about what the music said? . . . Actually, that Jesus-relationship that they were talking about tonight is the most important relationship I have in my life, too." Teenagers need to know how to use a meeting, because it creates a great opportunity to talk with a friend about Jesus Christ.

Here is one question that helps open the door after a meeting: "Have you ever felt like something's missing?" Or more directly, depending on the environment, encourage teenagers to ask their friends, "Has anyone ever shown you what the Bible says about how to have a relationship with God? They haven't? Wow! Well, someone did that for me, and I would love to do that with you."

Another way to get started is to *write a letter* to the friend. Some people often communicate better through writing, because the person speaking is not interrupted. Also, a friend will often consider it more, because he or she doesn't have to think of a verbal response while reading. Some young people will be able to do with a letter what they could not do verbally.

Our Christian kids owe every close non-Christian friend a chance to hear about Jesus before that graduation door slams, before his or her heart gets any harder. We can help our young warriors say it, write it, or have a quality place to bring a friend to hear someone else say it—but failure to tell about Jesus is too expensive. They have to do the telling . . . we have to help them know how. The coach is then helping his or her players win the victory that matters most.

A Friend to tell about . . . a friend to tell it to—the missing person in this tale of three people is the decisive link . . .

The Friend to Do the Telling

It all comes down to one young follower of Jesus Christ, standing between his Friend in heaven and his lost friend on earth. On one side there's a Friend named Jesus to tell about, and on the opposite side is a friend who doesn't know about Him, who needs to be told. What's missing is a bridge—someone to bring them together. The Person who did the dying and the person He died for—their getting together is in the hands of a Christian young person who knows them both.

As their spiritual coach, it is our responsibility to issue the challenge: "Would you be willing to take your Friend Jesus in heaven with one hand, and your friend on earth with the other hand, and be the one to bring them together? Christ has done His part on the Cross, and your friend desperately needs to know what Jesus died to do. Now it's up to you."

All that remains is a life-saving commitment on the part of that Christian teenager. Tenderly, prayerfully, the leader provides an opportunity for that young warrior to make this commitment— "I will do whatever it takes to bring my friend, (fill in the blank), to heaven with me." It is the greatest possible difference anyone can make in the life of someone they care about.

A YOUNG ARMY

A young army. That is what the Commander has come looking for. They are most strategically positioned to help fight the battle for a generation. But many have been sleeping comfortably in the cocoon of their youth group.

They need a mission they can own. It may begin in a rescue mission, an urban neighborhood, a senior citizens' facility, a youth choir. The mission may lead to a prayer breakfast, prayer triplets, a Christian club. But ultimately they must own the most personal mission of all—the spiritual rescue of a friend who is without Jesus.

The vision of what these sleeping warriors could be must begin in the heart of their leader—and spread from his heart to theirs. That leader will pray with them and for them . . . give them the "want to" and the "how to" they need . . . provide a climate of encouragement and motivation.

And if God makes a fire from the spark provided by the leader, what once was a youth group will become an army. Sleeping warriors will sleep no more. They will be wide awake and making a difference—soldiers in a battle that will matter forever.

13

Conclusion: Just Before You Join the Battle . . .

I f last week was typical, about 200 young people between the ages of 15 and 24 died in car crashes. Another 155 were murdered. And 90 killed themselves. Apart from a murder of a student by another at Johns Hopkins University, those deaths weren't in the news. . . . Why? Because they are so commonplace."

USA Today columnist Michael Gartner wrote this sobering commentary, which called this deadly scenario "outrageous" and "perplexing." After exploring more startling statistics about the loss of our young people, the writer issues, in essence, a call to arms: "We can't do anything until we acknowledge the numbers and treat them with the same outrage we find in war. . . . Until then, nothing will happen. And our sons and daughters will go on dying."[1]

A war mentality—that is what this secular columnist calls for as the appropriate response to the needs of our kids. And he sees their situation as literally being life-or-death. He is not alone. Educators, politicians, parents, social workers—many people seem to realize that there is, indeed, *a battle raging for a generation . . . and the winner owns the future.*

But ultimately it should be the people of God who see the battle most clearly, who respond with the greatest sense of urgency. It is the church that realizes that the issue is greater than teenage mortality—it is about the danger of being lost *eternally*. It is the church that knows that violence and suicide and drinking and sexual promiscuity are only the *symptoms*—that the real *problems* can only be solved by a right relationship with our Creator. And it is the church that *has the hope* these young people are looking for!

In his book *Generation Next*, George Barna observes that "about three-quarters of all people who have consciously, intentionally, and personally chosen to embrace Jesus Christ as their Savior did so before their 18th birthday." He follows with the disturbing discovery that "churches spend the vast majority of their evangelistic dollars (more than 70 percent of it, by some of our preliminary research) on trying to penetrate the adult market. After decades and decades of such toil, we can confidently announce the results: such efforts bear little fruit."[2]

On Wall Street or in any business venture, it obviously pays to invest in efforts that will get a good return. With reaching young people for Christ, we have an assignment that *does* bear fruit. The ground in young hearts is still soft enough for spiritual seed to take root . . . the scar tissue is not yet there to choke the seed . . . and a transformed teenager still has a whole life ahead to live for Christ. If you feel inadequate for God's assignment, you are in wonderful company! Moses, Gideon, Peter, Timothy—they are all people who struggled with their adequacy but whom God used mightily. If God has laid this burden on your heart, then He will empower and embolden you to carry it out. And you can lean on the promise that has sustained me through more than thirty years of reaching young people—"The one who calls you is faithful and he will do it" (1 Thessalonians 5:24).

THE VICTORY FACTOR

What does William Shakespeare have to do with the battle for a generation? Not much—except for the true story he dramatized in *Henry V*. It points us to the decisive factor in our battle for the lives of young people. The scene is the night before battle; the British Army will go to battle against the French at Agincourt the next morning. But the British soldiers are weary, sick—and outnumbered four to one! It looks like an unwinnable battle. Late that night, a hooded figure arrives at their encampment. He begins to make his way through the British lines, encouraging and challenging the soldiers. Eventually, the soldiers find out who their mysterious visitor is—it is Edward IV, the king himself! The next day the larger, stronger French Army is routed by the British. What made the difference in the outcome of the battle? *The presence of the king.*

As people who can see the battle raging for a generation of young people, we look out at a scene that appears overwhelming. The enemy is bombarding kids with media and money we cannot begin to match. He has a generation marching to his deadly music. And the needs of kids seem so complex . . . their distance from God and His ways so great . . . their "cool" so hard to get through. Worst of all, the army of those who are willing to fight for young people is so small compared to the number of kids to reach and the forces of darkness. On the eve of battle, we seem to be so outnumbered, so outgunned.

Except for the One who is walking among us, His troops. It is the *King Himself*—King Jesus, King of kings and Lord of lords. This is *His* battle to win. The decisive difference in this battle for the young people in our community is *the presence of the King in the midst of His army.*

Centuries ago, God's ancient people stood on the threshold of the Promised Land, on the edge of a great victory. But spies brought back reports of "people of great size." They said, "We seemed like grasshoppers in our own eyes" (Number 13:32–33). Like us preparing to take some ground back from Satan, they felt intimidated by the challenges—so much so that they turned back and spent forty years wandering in circles in the wilderness.

It was Joshua who understood the *real* odds in their fight. He challenged them to "not be afraid . . . their protection is gone, but *the Lord is with us*" (Numbers 14:9, italics added). Joshua's battle assessment ought to be ours as we go to spiritual war—the Lord is with us. And whatever is bigger than we are—*He* is bigger than it is! We can dare to launch an all-out, "Desert Storm" offensive to capture the hearts of the kids in our area—because of the conquering presence of our King.

He is, in fact, planning one final victorious sweep across Battlefield Earth before His personal return. The prophet Joel predicted it, and Peter underscored that prophecy on the Day of Pentecost. It suggests major spiritual victories—through a young army.

" 'In the last days,' God says, 'I will pour out My Spirit on all people. Your sons and daughters will prophesy, your young men will see visions . . .'" (Acts 2:17).

The last—and greatest—Spirit-move across this planet will come just before Jesus returns . . . and it seems as if it will be led by "your sons and daughters . . . your young men." There's a mighty work coming, and young people may be leading the charge!

With so many signs pointing to those "last days," that promise is a powerful encouragement for those of us fighting the battle for a generation. These young people to whom we are bringing Christ's love and hope could be part of that final, world-rocking *Jesus generation*. What a time to be fighting for young lives in Jesus' name!

THE WINNING MESSAGE

An old hymn says, "Tell me the story of Jesus." Modern young people might not like the hymn, but those words could be the cry of their soul. They are not institution people who care about rituals, religion, or rules. They are not abstract people who are looking for beliefs—or even truth. They are *story* people who learn most readily from stories. They are *spiritual* people who know instinctively that the answers are from something bigger than themselves. And they are *people* people who are in search of ultimate relationship. Of all the religions of the world, Christianity alone is all about a *person,* not a morality. Our lifestyle is the outgrowth of a love *relationship*. So—perhaps more than any North American kids in history—this generation needs to hear *the stories of Jesus!* Tell them the Gospel stories of what Jesus did, how He treated people, what He expected of people, how He changed people. Salvation is about a relationship with this *Jesus* . . . devotions is about spending time with *Jesus* . . . sin is about hurting *Jesus* . . . witnessing is telling about your relationship with *Jesus*. Keep bringing young people back to Jesus—He is everything a young person's heart is crying for.

THE PRICE OF VICTORY

Willing leaders need to pay the price for this mission. We need to *pay the price in prayer.* We have no right to enter this war in any other position than on our knees.

We need to *pay the price of purity.* We cannot reach into a battle against this kind of darkness if we are flirting with the darkness ourselves. In 2 Samuel 22:25, did David say, "The Lord has rewarded me according to my charisma . . . my spiritual accomplishments . . . my spiritual reputation . . . my abilities . . . my connections . . . ?" No, David said, "The Lord has rewarded me according to my righteousness, according to *my cleanness* in his sight" (italics added).

God is not looking for someone charismatic, brilliant, or clever. He is looking for someone clean. Anyone could be that person, but few people are willing. People need to know that the minute anyone steps up to say, "I'm going to go after this generation for Christ," he or she will have a target on his or her back that says, "He must be stopped. She must be stopped." That target will be from the Prince of Darkness. He wants the church to sleep through this war, to sleepwalk through the battle for a generation and let him have this generation uncontested. So, if you step up and say, "I will be a missionary and do what I can to make a difference," you can expect to be an enemy target.

We do not have to fear him, though, because greater is He who is in us than he who is in the world. But we do need to aggressively attack the sin in our lives. We cannot afford to give the enemy anything to work with, so we must keep paying the price of prayer and purity.

We need to *pay the price of passion.* It's expensive to carry around a broken heart, because all of a sudden, we're not just in a profession.

In a pastors' gathering I sat in on, the pastors were saying, "There's a whole new generation of people coming into Christian work whose first questions are, 'What's the benefit package, and how many weeks of vacation do I have?'" It's nice to have a benefit package, and vacation is important to keep from burning out, but those are the questions of someone with a profession, not a passion. If a person has a broken heart, it drives him to keep fighting, "benefits" or not, results or not, recognition or not.

THE HEART OF THE SAVIOR

In one of her diaries, missionary Amy Carmichael tells the story of looking out her window at the tamarind trees in India and picturing Jesus in the garden. Part of Amy's ministry was a vision to go in and rescue the little boys and girls who were being used as temple slaves and bring them to Christ. She had much opposition from the culture and even from some other missionaries. But she had real passion for that ministry.

She said the thing that kept her going was that sometimes she would look out her window and imagine that she saw Jesus kneeling as He did in the Garden of Gethsemane, not by an olive tree, but by one of the tamarind trees. She said, "I pictured myself going out there to see what He was doing. And when I went out there, I found that He was crying and sobbing over those boys and girls. I realized there was only one thing I could do. Kneel down next to Him and join Him in His tears. I cried for them, too."

Our Savior looked over His city of Jerusalem and wept. I believe today He looks over a generation and weeps at how lost they are, but how ready they are, and that no one is going out to get them.

As concerned adults, will we kneel down next to our Savior and shed some tears with Him over these young people? Perhaps He will even move us to pray like the great reformer, John Knox, who asked God to, "Give me Scotland or I die." As you catch the heartbeat of Jesus, you may find yourself praying, "Give me this high school, this junior high, this neighborhood. Give me this piece of ground for You, Lord, or I die."

When you begin to pray like that, your life days will be too short, and you will have had your last boring day! You will be a powerful instrument in your Master's hands, willing to pay the price of prayer, purity, and passion.

Dwight Eisenhower said, "There are no victories at discount prices." It will cost us, but we will ultimately win.

With the battle raging for the souls of our kids, each of us— as individuals, as churches, as organizations—has only two choices: to *join* the battle or *forfeit* a generation to the darkness.

So, in the unbeatable name of Jesus, we go to rescue young people who do not know Him and to summon to battle those who do. The time is short . . . the need is urgent . . . the mission is clear. In the words of Amy Carmichael, "We will have all eternity to celebrate our victories, but only a few short hours to win them."[3]

We are in those few short hours.

---

1. Michael Gartner, "Young Jessica, You're Not Alone," *USA Today*, 16 April 1996, 11A.
2. George Barna, *Generation Next* (Ventura, Calif.: Regal, 1996), 77.
3. Elisabeth Elliot, *A Chance to Die: The Life and Legacy of Amy Carmichael* (Grand Rapids: Revell, 1987).

RESOURCES FOR YOUTH MINISTRY FROM RON HUTCHCRAFT

VIDEO: *Sex at its Best! A Positive Morality for Today's Youth*
Hosted by Ron Hutchcraft

A high-energy, fast-moving video, designed to present today's youth with a life-changing, love-saving challenge, with a plan for "how to keep sex special." But more significantly, Ron presents an opportunity for young people to surrender their lives to Jesus Christ. Leader's Guide included. Available at your local Christian bookstore, or call Gospel Films, (800) 253–0413.

VIDEO: *Reaching Contemporary Youth (15 volumes)*
with Ron Hutchcraft

A comprehensive, practical training series for adults involved in the evangelism, discipling, and counseling of young people. In a classroom setting, Ron further develops the themes explored in this book, *Battle for a Generation.* Available through Ron Hutchcraft Ministries, P.O. Box 1818, Wayne NJ 07474, (201) 696–2161.

EVANGELISM BOOKLET: Yours for Life
by Ron Hutchcraft

In this mini-booklet, Ron presents the core Gospel message of Jesus Christ in non-religious language. An ideal, contemporary witnessing tool for all ages. Contact American Tract Society, P.O Box 462008, Garland, TX 75046–2008, (214) 276–9400.

BOOK: *Letters from the College Front*
Guys' Edition by Ron Hutchcraft & Doug Hutchcraft
Girls' Edition by Ron Hutchcraft & Lisa Hutchcraft Whitmer

Letters from the "front" in which high school graduates will find helpful advice, biblical principles, and straight-forward discussion on important issues and situations related to college life. Available at your local Christian bookstore, or call Baker Book House, (800) 877–2665.

RADIO BROADCAST: *"Alive! with Ron Hutchcraft!"*

This weekly, one-hour program features issues young people care about, a live studio audience of teenagers, contemporary Christian music, drama, and biblical straight talk that hits home. Ron concludes every program at the Cross and introduces teenagers to a relationship with Jesus Christ with a clear presentation of the Gospel. For more information, contact your local Christian radio station, or Ron Hutchcraft Ministries, P.O. Box 1818, Wayne NJ 07474, (201) 696–2161.

INTERNET — *Ron Hutchcraft Ministries*

Additional resources and information from Ron Hutchcraft Ministries can be found on the Internet: http://www.hutchcraft.com. RHM is part of the *Gospel Communications Network* (http://www.gospelcom.net), where you can find several leading national youth organizations on-line, featuring an endless wealth of additional resources for youth ministry.

For further information, please contact:

Ron Hutchcraft Ministries
P.O. Box 1818 Wayne NJ 07474–1818
(201) 696–2161; FAX: (201) 694–1182
Internet: http://www.hutchcraft.com

Moody Press, a ministry of Moody Bible Institute,
is designed for education, evangelization, and edification.
If we may assist you in knowing more about Christ
and the Christian life, please write us without obligation:
Moody Press, c/o MLM, Chicago, Illinois 60610.